A THIRST that Never CEASES

JUDY OWENS

ISBN 978-1-63885-210-0 (Paperback)
ISBN 978-1-63885-211-7 (Digital)

Covenant Books, Inc.
11661 Hwy 707
Murrells Inlet, SC 29576
www.covenantbooks.com

"Mom! Wake up! You are talking in your sleep again!" screamed Janice as she attempted to wake Rose from what appeared to be another horrific nightmare. "Mom, you really need to talk to someone about your dreams. Maybe a professional can help you recall, as well as understand the reason for your dreams."

Rose looked at her daughter like she was the one with a problem. She couldn't wrap her thoughts around why her daughter woke her up when she was having the best rest of her life.

"What do you mean I was talking in my sleep? Talking in my sleep doesn't mean I have a professional problem. I was sleeping peacefully before you woke me up. Are you sure I'm the one who needs to talk to a professional?"

"Mom, you were moaning soft screams as you tossed and turned in a defensive manner with stretched out arms as your hands moved in a windmill motion. You were obviously fighting something or someone in your sleep."

Rose, a middle-aged woman born in the early sixties, was very attractive for her age. Her skin was a golden bronze with no blemish outside of a few small facial freckles. Her physical appearance looked fit for a small-framed stature of five feet four inches.

Rose birthed two children in her first marriage, a son and a daughter. She birthed a daughter in her second marriage. Her eldest daughter, Janice, moved back home after Rose divorced her second husband. Janice felt it was her obligation, as the only unmarried child, to care for her mom after experiencing her mom going through a very emotional divorce.

Janice never felt her stepfather was good for her mom. She felt her mom could have married someone more educated and professionally skilled. Janice felt maybe these flaws wouldn't have been so bad if her stepfather, Craig, was a handsome man. Although Janice was six years of age when her mom married Craig, she never felt her stepdad was a great father figure in her life. She always felt he had a better relationship with her brother, James Jr., and her younger sister, Craig's biological daughter, Chloe. James Jr. was called JJ for short. JJ was eleven years of age when Rose married Craig. Janice couldn't understand why Craig would cling to her brother like he was his blood son but always seemed to resent her. She understood his reason for being close to his only blood child, Chloe, but often wondered what she had done to cause him to not like her.

Now that Rose was awaken early on a Saturday, she decided to get an early start, taking care of some errands on her to-do list. *Let's see*, thought Rose, *after a quick thirty-minute jog around the neighborhood with Josey, I need to drop off Josey for grooming, pick up my dry cleaning, stop at the coffee shop for a quick breakfast before heading to the farmer's market, and finally, pick up Josey before meeting my best friend, Barbara, of forty years for lunch. Thank goodness the café is only ten minutes from home.*

Rose realized how tight her morning scheduled had become. She was looking forward to having girl talk with Barbara. It had been over a month since they met up for lunch. Rose and Barbara's once-a-month meeting was a form of refuge for both women. They were able to discuss their victories, problems, and concerns in a safe environment, among two friends, without feeling like they were being judged or prosecuted for their thoughts or actions.

After Rose returned home from running errands, she realized it was 12:50 p.m. She texted Barbara to let her know she would be ten minutes late. She needed a few minutes to freshen up before heading to the café.

Barbara and Rose greeted each other with a hug. The waitress greeted the two ladies, "Welcome back. A table for two is open near the back, or would you two prefer to wait for your usual table near the window?"

"The back would be okay," Barbara replied. She knew Rose wasn't particular about where they sat.

After the ladies gave the waitress their usual order, grilled chicken breast, string bean fries with a glass of red wine, Barbara asked Rose, "So how are things going? Divorce looks good on you. You look rested and happy."

Rose smirked a half smile as she hunched her shoulders.

"What is that look about?" asked Barbara.

"Well, where do I begin? A lot has happened in the past month," Rose paused before continuing to speak. "I feel happier than I have been in years. My home is peaceful. Janice and I are coexisting well together. She has been a big help to me since moving back home. Chloe and JJ have committed to having family dinner every fourth Sunday. My business is flourishing. Life couldn't be any better."

"So why the long face?" asked Barbara.

"Well, I feel Janice and I have mastered how to camouflage our emotions with an outside projection of wellness." Rose paused as she thought about what she had just said. It made her realize she had mastered how to deceive herself, as well as others.

Barbara looked complexed as she searched for the right words in expressing her thoughts. She did not want Rose to perceive her thoughts as negative or as an attack of her spiritual beliefs, especially since Rose had never judge her as other Christians have for being an openly gay woman. Throughout the years, Rose had endured a lot of animosity from other parishioners because of her friendship with Barbara. For this reason, Barbara withheld from sharing her thoughts by asking Rose, "How is Janice? Is she still having difficulties dealing with James Sr.'s death?"

Rose looked away before speaking. "Yes, she is. Although it has been years since his demise, she might still be grieving or still be angry at him."

Barbara had to find the words to express what was on her mind. *Well, here goes forty years of friendship*, she thought as she began to speak, "Rose, I believe Janice's and your emotional stability would be enriched by discussing horrific life events with a professional. Most of my life, I have talked with a professional regarding life as an openly gay woman. As you know, it was not easy for my Christian parents to accept my sexuality. You were my only friend for years; yet I haven't had the courage to share with you that I have been talking to a professional psychologist most of my life. Nor have I told anyone how I nearly succeeded in committing suicide as a teen. Throughout the years, I felt guilty in not completely sharing what I was going through with you. I was so afraid of you changing how you see me. It was my psychologist that helped me to see your true friendship. My thoughts were so tainted by the hate I was receiving to trust anybody 100 percent, even if this person was a good friend.

"For years, I thought my parents' love was conditional. I thought their love was conditioned upon me not being a gay woman; and because I couldn't give them what they wanted, they couldn't give me what I needed, which is love. During a family counseling session with my psychologist, my parents told me that God hated gay people, and this is his reason for destroying the land of Sodom and Gomorrah. They said that God will destroy me as well. I was so angry with them that I blurted out what you had said to me when I asked you why you didn't judge or hate me the way other Christian have, why you are my friend when God hates me. I asked you if you were afraid of being punished by God. You said to me, 'God doesn't hate people. He hates some of the things that people do. The things that people do that God hates is called sin.' You said that God understands why people sin. This is the reason he made provision for people's sins. People were born into sin. I asked you why God hates what he created in us. You said it's because he did not create sin in us. He created man and woman in his likeness, which is love.

"He also created man and women with free will in their decision-making. Upon the creation of man and woman, God gave a specific command, which is to not eat from the tree of the knowledge of good and evil. This command was compromised with disobedience through free will. Eating from the tree of the knowledge of good and evil opened men and women's knowledge not only to the good God had created in them but also to the evil God had not created in them. You said that God destroyed the evil that was in the heart of men and women in the land of Sodom and Gomorrah because they refused to repent and change from their evil ways. You said that you prefer to use your free will to operate in God's likeness, which is love. And that you were not the god of people; therefore, it was not your position to judge people's sin.

"My parents became so angry at you when I told them what you said to me. Their anger caused them to question your friendship to me, and when it was exposed in the church that I was gay, my parents spread lies about you to give the impression that you were the reason why I was sexually confused. Please forgive me for not telling you years ago that it was my parents' fault why many parishioners treated you badly for being my friend."

Rose felt a little hurt that her best friend did not share this information with her sooner, but she understood her reason. Rose comforted Barbara by saying, "No need to apologize for your parents' actions. I can only now imagine the magnitude of what you were going through. It is much larger than our discussions throughout the years. The sessions with the psychologist had to help because your relationship with your parents appeared to be okay for years."

Barbara took Rose's hand and placed it in her hand as she looked her in the eyes. "Rose, please do not question our friendship because I did not share with you sooner my family issues. Now that I have healed from the pain and hurt of how I was treated because of who I am, I can freely talk about it without feeling like I want to end my life.

"You are correct in your observation. My relationship with my parents started improving in my late twenties and began to flourish in my forties. As you can see, it took a while to get there. Both my parents, now in their late eighties, love me unconditionally. I owe this to God in opening their hearts and minds, as well as the Christian psychologist who became our life coach throughout this journey."

Rose's eyes sparkled with relief as she asked her friend, "How can I find a good psychologist with biblical principles to coach me and my daughter?"

Barbara offered to give Rose a referral to a psychologist she worked with professionally at the Children's Hospital. "Rose, I will email you on Monday morning Dr. Ruth Gordon's contact information. Dr. Ruth has worked over twenty years as a child psychologist for Children's Hospital of Clarksdale and seventeen years as a psychologist for the Women's Health Clinic here in town. Although she is not the psychologist who counseled me and my parents, I know her to be good in her profession. I have seen many of her patients have rapid improvements in their physical health due to the psychological improvement of their mind."

"Barbara, thank you for being open and candid with me today. This is what I cherish about our friendship. I am truly blessed to have you as a friend. I am looking forward to contacting Dr. Ruth. Your experience has opened my mind to counseling. All my life in church, the preacher would say, 'The only psychiatrist you need is Jesus. Cast your cares on him. He is your doctor. He is your lawyer. He is your psychiatrist.' Yet throughout the years, I have gone to doctors and lawyers but thought it was a taboo to go see a psychologist or psychiatrist.

"Well, unless we plan on staying for dinner, I think it's time for us to give up our table. Let's promise to not wait nearly two months before we meet again"

"I promise!" Barbara gladly shouted with a big smile.

The ladies hugged as they exited the café and went their separate ways.

Upon arriving home, Rose called out Janice's name to see if she was home. Janice came from the family room, carrying a bowl of popcorn and a glass of soda. Josey came running from the family room as well. Josey jumped on Rose over and over again, showing her excitement to see her. Rose expressed to Janice how she would like for them to have dinner together tonight to discuss a suggestion Barbara had made at lunch. Janice agreed then asked, "How is Ms. Barbara?"

"She is well. It was good seeing her. I feel like I made a new friend today. I am still wrapping my mind around our discussion at lunch. I'm not at liberty to share, but I can tell you this: God is amazing. His timing is impeccable, always on time. I was truly blessed and enlightened today and filled with faith that we will be okay. This, too, shall pass. With that being said, let's talk at dinner."

Rather than spending hours in the kitchen cooking, Rose decided to order dinner from her favorite restaurant. She ordered the chef's special, which consisted of baked salmon with lemon butter sauce, grilled asparagus, and baby red potatoes.

The doorbell rang, and Janice called out, "Mom, the delivery order is here." Rose entered the foyer with cash in her hand.

As she tipped the driver, Janice carried the food into the dining room and proceeded in setting the dining table for dinner. As Janice was placing plates and utensils on the placemats, Rose joined her with a glass of soda in one hand and a glass of red wine in the other. As they sat for dinner, Rose grabbed Janice's hands. "Let's go back to our roots. Let's pray before we eat."

Janice nodded her head in agreement.

"Heavenly Father, in the name of your Son and our Savior, Jesus Christ, we ask that you bless this food and the people who put care into preparing this meal. Thank you, God."

Janice closed Rose's prayer with an amen.

Janice hummed as she swallowed a piece of salmon. Rose looked at Janice with a smile. "I knew you would enjoy it.

"I want to talk about our buried emotional issues that manifest in the presence of others. Yet we deny these issues' existence. For instance, before you moved back home, I did not know I was tossing and talking in my sleep. Obviously, I have some buried issues because in my thoughts, all is well. I want to heal my mind. I do not want these buried issues to grow into something toxic that would lead to psychological or health issues."

"You said *our* buried issues," declared Janice.

"Yes, I did. This is because I, and others, have noticed your reactions to conversations dealing with James Sr.'s lifestyle preceding his death."

Janice's demeanor shifted to one of sorrow and hurt.

"Also, you have always believed Craig had ill intentions toward you regardless of his outward expressions of kindness and attention he equally gave to you, JJ, and Chloe.

"Barbara worked with a psychologist who is also a Christian life coach. Her name is Dr. Ruth Gordon. I think we both can benefit from talking to someone who is a professional with biblical principles. I think we should set up a consultation with Dr. Ruth and, in the meantime, pray for our hearts and minds to receive and recognize truth. I would like for us both to be prepared in making a discussion about counseling after the consultation."

"I trust you, Mom. I believe you are observing a behavior in me that I don't know exists. I am looking forward to hearing what Dr. Ruth has to say."

Rose kissed Janice on the forehead as she cleared the table. "It has been a long day. I will be in my room reading if you need me," declared Rose.

Janice nodded with acknowledgement as she headed back to the family room.

Monday morning, Rose woke up at 5:30 a.m. She grabbed her jogging wear and sneakers from her walk-in closet. She called Josey's name as she headed toward the kitchen. Josey came running, wagging her tail with excitement. She put Josey's body collar and leash on her. Josey jumped with excitement.

"Let's go," says Rose as she opened the back door. She and Josey jogged around the neighborhood for thirty minutes before heading back home.

Rose refreshed Josey's water and food bowl before heading back upstairs to her room. She showered and dressed in a nice business pants suit. Janice was preparing for her clinical intern shift as a physical therapist. Rose yelled upstairs to Janice, "Have a good day!" before heading out the door.

Rose's business partner, Charles, had opened the office prior to her arrival at 7:55 a.m. She greeted him before heading to the break room for coffee. As brokers of a realtor company, Rose and her business partner oversaw several real estate salespersons, as well as supervise their administration staff.

Charles had brought in donuts and bagels with cream cheese. Rose grabbed a blueberry bagel to have with her coffee. After turning on the computer in her office, Rose noticed Barbara had emailed her at 8:05 a.m. She jotted down Dr. Ruth's contact information on a piece of paper. She sent Barbara a quick email, thanking her for the information.

Rose contemplated if she should call or email Dr. Ruth. She decided to introduce herself in an email with a follow-up phone call.

By 9:00 a.m., Rose had emailed Dr. Ruth, giving her a little background on how she obtained her contact information, as well as a brief explanation as to why she was contacting her. She expressed to Dr. Ruth that she would call her office to schedule a consultation. Rose and Janice's appointment was scheduled for the end of the week at 3:00 p.m. Rose was grateful the day and time of their appointment fit Janice's schedule. Janice interned half days on Fridays.

Rose and Janice were nervous about their appointment. They arrived twenty minutes early. The receptionist called them in five minutes after completing the new patient documents. Rose did most of the talking with brief interjections from Janice. Dr. Ruth remained silent as she observed the constant change in their demeanors. After thirty minutes, Dr. Ruth gave a brief background on herself. She suggested a separate weekly one-hour counseling for each of them, as well as a monthly family group session with the two. Rose and Janice agreed to Dr. Ruth's suggestion. Consecutive one-hour sessions were set up for Rose and Janice each Friday.

On the ride home, Rose asked Janice how she felt about sharing with JJ and Chloe their decision to counsel with a psychologist. Janice expressed she wanted to be transparent with her siblings but was uncomfortable with talking about it. Rose assured Janice they would only be informed; her sessions are with Dr. Ruth only, not her siblings.

During the duration of the drive home, the two planned Sunday family dinner.

*****

Rose woke up early on Sunday to prepare for dinner. Because it was the first planned family dinner since the kids moved out the home, she wanted it to be perfect. It's important to make this day special for JJ's and Chloe's spouses as well. Rose knew the spouses play a key role in upholding the commitment of having family dinner every other Sunday.

Chloe married her high school sweetheart six months after graduating from college. They had been married for two years. She worked as an elementary teacher. Although she loved kids, she was not ready to have any of her own. Chloe's husband supported her decision to wait until their fifth wedding anniversary to consummate it with the hopes of becoming pregnant.

JJ had been married to his lovely wife, Grace, for five years. In the second year of their marriage, JJ and Grace gave birth to James Jackson III, whom everyone calls Trey for short.

On the ride home from Dr. Ruth's office, Rose and Janice agreed the theme of the dinner should be soul food family reunion. Janice was responsible for the entertainment, and Rose was responsible for preparing the meal. Rose decided to prepare the kids favorite soul food dishes. Her menu included collard greens with smoked turkey wings, mac 'n' cheese, candied yams, cornbread dressing with cranberry sauce, fried chicken and fish, and potato salad.

After leaving the farmer's market, Janice went next door to the farmer's bakery to pick up a dozen of assorted mini cupcakes. She ordered three carrot cupcakes, three red velvet cupcakes, three cheesecake cupcakes, and three German chocolate cupcakes.

Upon arriving home, Rose called for Janice to come help her with the grocery. As they were unloading the car, Rose asked Janice how the entertainment was coming along. Janice answered, "All set. I was able to find a game store that carry many board games." Janice had purchased Monopoly, Checkers, Dominos, Twister, Charade, and Legos for Trey.

JJ and Chloe arrived around 3:00 p.m., within minutes of each other. Janice instructed everyone to gather in the family room, where a small tray of crackers with crab dip lay on a table.

Rose made her way from the kitchen to greet everyone. She expressed her happiness in seeing them as they embraced each other with hugs and kisses.

"Dinner will be ready in thirty minutes," Rose declared with tears in her eyes.

"Mom," called JJ with a smile, "the aroma of the food brings back memories as a kid." He began to verbally reminisce about their family gatherings during the holidays. Everyone laughed and giggled.

Rose excused herself. "I need to check on dinner."

JJ's wife, Grace, and Chloe offered to help. Rose asked if they would set the table as Janice set up the drinks.

"Trey and I will do what guys normally do while waiting on dinner: rush you all in our minds!" JJ shouted with laughter.

Rose's long dinner room table for ten fit the family of seven perfectly. With Rose at the head of the table, Janice sat on the right side of Rose. Next to Janice sat Chloe and her husband, Robert. JJ sat on the left side of Rose. Next to JJ sat his wife, Grace, and their son, Trey.

Rose asked JJ if he would bless the food in prayer. JJ asked everyone to bow their heads as he began to pray. There were shouts of "Amen!" around the table after JJ completed his prayer.

As the serving dishes were passed around the table for each to fill their plates, Rose let the family knew that she and Janice had a consultation with a psychologist who was also a Christian life coach.

JJ asked, "What bought about the decision to see a psychologist, and what is the outcome of the consultation?"

Rose gave brief details about her sleeping disorder that resulted in tossing, turning, and talking in her sleep. Janice spoke briefly about her insecurities.

"Janice and I agreed to counsel separately with Dr. Ruth," Rose replied to JJ's question.

Chloe asked, "Do you two feel this psychologist would help you both find the root cause, as well as guide you with biblical principles in gaining spiritual and mental wellness?"

Rose and Janice replied at the same time, "Yes."

"You have my support," declared Chloe.

JJ followed with, "You both have my support and blessing as well."

Trey shouted, "When do we get to eat some of that cake over there?" pointing at the long serving table near the wall. They all looked in the direction Trey was pointing and began to laugh.

"He is his father's son," Rose said while shaking her head.

"Let's have dessert so I can whip you all in a game of Charade," Janice bragged.

After a few hours of playing board games, JJ looked at the clock with amazement. "Wow, it's eight o'clock already. Time flies when you are having fun."

JJ reminded everyone that tomorrow is Monday. They all agreed it was time to call it a night. Rose and Janice packaged carry-home containers with food for JJ and Chloe. They all expressed how much they enjoyed themselves, and vowed to bring a dish to the next family dinner so Rose wouldn't have to cook a feast. Rose agreed. Janice and Rose cleaned up the kitchen after everyone left then headed upstairs to bed.

*****

Rose arrived ten minutes early for her first counsel meeting with Dr. Ruth. Rose, this being her first time, didn't know how counseling worked and therefore felt a little uncomfortable. She began to question herself if this was a good decision. After reminiscing about her conversation with Barbara, she noticed the nervousness was gone.

Dr. Ruth came out personally to call Rose into her office. She asked Rose to have a seat on the couch. Rose observed the room was not the same office where she and Janice met with Dr. Ruth for the consultation. The initial meeting office was large. It had a long cherry wood desk with three French conventional chairs facing the desk. Along the walls were two cherry wood bookshelves filled with books, framed pictures, and awards.

Rose noticed how warm and cozy the counseling room was as she waited on Dr. Ruth to get situated. The room was filled with pastel colors. The only furniture was a couch with two end tables, a center coffee table, and a large French conventional chair that faced the couch. In the corner of the room was a small refrigerator. One end table was next to the couch, while the other end table was next to the chair.

Dr. Ruth took a seat in the chair after picking up the laptop from the end table next to the chair. She offered Rose a bottle of water from the refrigerator. Rose declined but thanked her for the offer. There was an awkward moment of silence. Dr. Ruth looked at

Rose before saying, "There is nothing to be nervous about. We are going to talk about life. Let's start with your first marriage. Feel free to verbalize your life story."

Rose thought out loud, "Well, let's see. I was working at a law firm as a paralegal when I met my first husband, James. The firm was looking to hire and decided to set up interviews with potential candidates who had recently passed their bar exam. In walked James into the law firm as my coworker and I researched through legal books and documents for a case one of the lawyers were working on. He was six feet three inches tall, looking finer than wine in his three-piece suit. My coworker Brenda and I were hypnotized by his presence. We stared without blinking for sixty seconds. James turned in our direction, smiled, and nodded his head as he walked toward the reception desk. The receptionist asked him to have a seat as she informed the attorney that his ten o'clock appointment had arrived.

"During lunch, Brenda and I discussed if we thought James had the job or not. Not only was Brenda my coworker, she was my best friend from high school. We both went to paralegal school together. We were also roommates. We shared a two-bedroom, two-bathroom apartment. In those days, it was cheaper to split the rent on a two-bedroom than separately rent a one-bedroom. We both felt so blessed to find jobs with the same firm fresh out of school.

"Brenda and I did not find out James was hired until a week later when he came back into the firm carrying a small box of personal items. Although Brenda and I were young, we both knew and discussed it was not good to date anyone where we worked.

"One day while at home, six months after James was hired, Brenda asked me why James was always talking to me at work. I looked at her in a state of shock because he talked to everyone in the office. I told her, 'I don't understand your question.' I asked Brenda, 'Was he not supposed to talk to me?' Brenda blurted out, 'I think he likes you.' I disagreed with Brenda because he never told me he liked me or asked me out on a date. But two weeks after our conversation, James stopped me at work as I was walking to my car. He asked me how I felt about dating someone I work with. I told him it was not good because it could affect the professional relationship. He then asked how I felt about socializing with someone I work with after work hours. I told James I was okay with it as long as the relationship was strictly platonic."

Dr. Ruth injected, "Did you find James attractive?"

"Yes," Rose replied.

"Were you concerned socializing with someone who wanted to date you and who you find attractive would lead to something more than platonic?" asked Dr. Ruth.

"I thought about it for a quick second but told myself James understood from our conversation that I was not looking to take the relationship outside of a friendship among coworkers. After all, I socialized with others in the office after work."

After Rose's remark, Dr. Ruth asked, "How did your relationship with James became more than platonic?"

"Our initial socializing after work started as a group with other coworkers. We all would occasionally meet in the bar area of a local restaurant for happy hour. After a couple of months of socializing with James among the group, I allowed my guard to come down and no longer felt our friendship was in threat of changing into an intimate relationship. The one day after leaving the bar, James asked to walk me to my car. It was dark outside, so I agreed. When I got in my car, James leaned in and kissed me. To my surprise, I kissed him back. James smiled and nodded as he told me to have a good night. That night, I couldn't sleep from thinking about what happened. I realized I was harboring feelings for James that I had suppressed. I felt like I had awakened within myself a sleeping giant with one kiss. I began to ask myself, how do I close this emotional door? I felt like my entire being was filled, in an instant, from one kiss with emotions I did not know was in me.

"The next day at work was awkward. I tried to avoid James. I had no one to talk to about the situation. I couldn't talk to Brenda because there was no way she would believe the kiss between James and me came as a surprise to me. Immediately after work, James called me at home. Brenda was out on a date with a guy she met two months ago. James and I talked about what happened. He told me how much he liked me and wanted to move our relationship from the friend's zone to dating. I had never felt so much bubbling inside for anyone, which made it hard for me to say no. I never had a serious boyfriend. I allowed my emotions to guide my decisions with James from that point of the kiss to the end of our relationship.

"James and I started secretly dating. I was falling deep fast. Three months after dating, James asked to come to my apartment. He knew I shared an apartment with Brenda. He asked if Brenda's boyfriend comes to our apartment. I could hear the hurt in his voice when I said yes. So knowing that Brenda was going to be on a date on Friday with her boyfriend, I told James to come on Friday. James arrived on time. I poured us both a glass of wine. As we cuddled on the couch, watching TV, Brenda walked through the door. I jumped. She looked back and forth from me to James. James's greeting of hi to Brenda was met with a look of grimness from her to him. Brenda headed to her bedroom without saying a word. James asked me, 'What is that all about?' As I was explaining to James why I kept our relationship a secret from Brenda, she reentered the living room wearing a sexy black negligee. She told James, 'This is what you are missing by choosing Rose over me.' I was so angry I began to cry. James stood up, looked at me, and said, 'Now I understand. We will talk later. Don't let this vex your spirit.' He kissed me then left.

"Brenda ran back to her bedroom. I could hear her crying. The next day, she apologized to me, and I gave her my thirty-day notice. Our relationship shifted from best friends to professional coworkers. James asked me to move in with him and I did. James and I eloped six months after living together, which was approximately a year and seven months after he walked into the firm for an interview.

"After marrying James, I submitted my two-week resignation to my boss. Brenda's boyfriend moved in with her. James and I gave birth to James Jr. two years after getting married. Our marriage prior to James Jr. was good. We were so in love with each other and showed it in affection every day. I became less affectionate after JJ was born. Going to night school and working a full shift at work and at home became very draining. I was tired all the time. James Sr. sought out the affection he was missing at home with other women. Adding this emotional hurt to my workload made things worse in my marriage.

"When JJ was four years old, I knew my marriage was in serious threat of dissolution. I thought having another child would save our marriage. James Sr. was furious when I told him we were pregnant. He asked me to have an abortion. Shortly after JJ's fifth birthday, when I was eight months pregnant, James Sr. served me with divorce papers. Janice was born a month later without her father to welcome her into this world."

Dr. Ruth took notes as Rose talked about her life. She intervened to let Rose know that her hour was up. She stated that next week, she would like for them to discuss Rose's emotional state after the dissolution of her marriage.

Rose passed Janice in the waiting room. Janice looked at her mom then asked if everything was okay. Rose put on a brave face, smiled at Janice, and said, "Yes, all is well."

Dr. Ruth came into the waiting room to call Janice into her office. Janice commented on the warmth and coziness of the room as she opened the bottle of water Dr. Ruth handed her. Janice asked Dr. Ruth if her mom was okay.

"Why do you ask?" Dr. Ruth replied.

"Well, she looked sad as she exited the office." Janice tried to smile but felt sad thinking of her mom.

Dr. Ruth asked Janice if it would be easier for her to come in before her mom. Janice thought for a brief moment then agreed with Dr. Ruth's suggestion. Dr. Ruth promised to have her secretary contact Rose about switching her counseling session with Janice's session time.

Janice, eager to get started, asked Dr. Ruth, "What are we going to talk about?"

"Tell me about your childhood. You can start at your earliest recollection."

Janice paused before speaking, "I recall, at the age of four, asking my mom, 'Who is my dad?'"

Dr. Ruth asked Janice, "Why did you ask your mom that question? Have you not seen your dad prior to age four?"

"No, I had never seen my dad. My brother JJ was always over his dad's house on the weekend. JJ's dad would come to the house and blow his car horn before JJ went running out the door. When Mom told me that JJ and I have the same dad, I asked my mom why I don't go over my dad's house on the weekends like JJ. Mom said Dad did not want to take a girl to do rough boys' things. She also said my dad thought it would be better if I stayed home and learned about girls' things with her. I asked my mom what boys' things were. She explained they were fishing, hiking, going to sport games, and playing sports. Then I said, 'Is coming in the house to say hi a girl thing?'

"'What do you mean?' Mom replied.

"I told Mom, 'Because my dad never come in the house to see me. He only blows his horn for JJ to come out the house.' My mom looked at me and began to cry. I told Mom that I was sorry I asked her that bad question. That I didn't want her to cry. Then Mom said that it was okay, and she would talk to my dad about coming in the house to say hi. Two days later, after JJ returned home, Mom went outside to talk with Dad. The back door was left open. I stood near the kitchen door when I heard Mom tell Dad, 'Janice is asking about her dad.' And Dad said, 'I told you that I did not want any more kids when you were pregnant with Janice. You should be happy I am paying child support for a child that should have been aborted.' Mom told Dad that he was not allowed to take JJ again until he came in the house to meet me, and that he had to be kind toward me. Dad said, 'I will see you in court,' then drove out the driveway."

Dr. Ruth asked Janice how she felt after overhearing her parents' conversation.

"I don't know. I did not know the meaning of what they were saying. I felt it wasn't good because my mom and dad sounded angry and were yelling. For a long time, JJ did not go over to dad's house on the weekends. JJ was angry with me because Dad told him that it was my fault. I did not understand what I had done wrong. After JJ told me it was my fault, I heard Mom talking on the phone with Ms. Barbara. Mom told Ms. Barbara that she was happy James Sr. agreed to her hosting JJ's tenth birthday party so that I could meet my dad and JJ could start going back to Dad's house on the weekend. I was so excited. I ran to tell JJ what I heard. JJ began to jump for joy and said he was sorry to me, and we hugged. Mom invited all of JJ's friends from school, and Dad invited all of JJ's friends on his basketball team.

"When my dad walked into Ms. Barbara backyard carrying a large gift-wrapped box, I knew he was my dad. I stared at him for a long time. He stared back at me. JJ interrupted our staring by running to him, shouting, "Dad!" Dad laid the gift box on the table then grabbed and hugged JJ. Tears came to my eyes, and JJ asked me why I was crying. I hunched my shoulders and said I don't know. Then my dad came over to me, and he grabbed my hand as he got on his knees. He told me that I was beautiful and looked like my grandmother, his mom. He hugged me for the first time. I couldn't stop crying. A tear fell down my dad's eyes as well. I then asked my dad if he was coming to my birthday party in three months. Dad said he wouldn't miss my fifth birthday.

"Ms. Barbara lived with a lady who she called her partner. As a kid, I did not know that *partner* was not her name but was her title. Ms. Barbara's cousin came to the party with his ten-year-old nephew. Her cousin's name was Craig. Craig and Mom talked a lot at the party. Dad looked angry every time he looked at Craig talking to Mom. After the party, Dad walked me, JJ, and Mom to the car as he pushed a cart with all of JJ's gifts. Dad asked me where I would like to have my birthday party, and I happily answered at the Disney Land. Dad promised to make it happen.

"After JJ's party, Dad came to the house every weekend to pick up JJ and visit me before taking JJ to his house. Sometimes he would take me and JJ for ice cream. Mom had bought me a pink princess dress with a silver tiara for my birthday. I was so happy to have my mom and dad celebrate my fifth birthday with me. Although my mom and dad did not have any conversations outside of asking and answering questions about me and JJ, we were all happy with each other. Until Dad overheard Mom talking on the phone, saying Craig asked her to marry him. Dad's tone began to change toward Mom. He no longer smiled when he saw her. Mom married Craig two months before JJ's eleventh birthday. Dad was so angry at Mom that he started binge drinking."

Dr. Ruth asked, "What is your understanding of binge drinking at age five?"

"I heard Mom say on the phone that she was scared of Dad taking me and JJ in his car because of his constant drinking and driving. Mom said Dad had to go to court because he has a DUI for binge drinking. I asked JJ what a DUI was. JJ searched DUI on the internet and said it was driving under the influence of a substance. I asked JJ what a substance was. He said alcohol or drugs. 'Can you drink alcohol?' I asked him.

"'Why do you need to know!' JJ shouted. I told him what I heard Mom say on the phone. 'Yes, alcohol is something a person drinks,' JJ replied. Although at the age of five, I did not fully understand, I knew that my dad had to go to court because he drank alcohol. Also, I knew that my dad did not come to my sixth birthday party because he was driving drunk and ran into a tree with his car. My dad was in the hospital for two weeks when he died of complications from injuries due to the car accident."

Dr. Ruth let Janice know that their time was up. She told Janice that she wanted to explore her thoughts and feelings about her dad's death in her next session. And as promised, Dr. Ruth had her secretary call Rose to ask her permission in switching her session time with Janice. Rose agreed with the switch and was grateful Dr. Ruth had observed Janice's emotional response to seeing her coming out of her session with a sad look. Rose felt she and Janice were in good hands with Dr. Ruth.

At home, Rose and Janice did not talk about their session with Dr. Ruth. They sat and watched TV together while making small talk about their week. Rose asked Janice her plans for the weekend.

"Well, let see. I plan on going to the art exhibition at the convention center with a couple of classmates. We would probably go walk the shorelines at the beach afterward."

"Good. I am happy to hear you are getting out the house for some enjoyment."

"What about you, Mom?"

"Oh, I plan on meeting Barbara for lunch."

"Mom, do you ever think about dating again?"

"No. I'm not ready. I need a few more sessions with Dr. Ruth before I add anymore complexity to my life."

Janice and Rose both laughed.

At lunch, Barbara asked Rose if she and Janice were adjusting well with Dr. Ruth.

"Yes, I feel comfortable sharing the sensitive period of my life with Dr. Ruth. Although Janice and I don't talk about our sessions with each other, I can tell she feels the same as me."

"That's good to hear, Rose. Keep in mind that life issues are not an overnight fix. It might take a year or two to really understand what has been suppressed and how it has affected your life choices."

"I agree with you, Barbara. I am looking forward to knowing the root cause of what is disrupting my sleep, and I am willing to follow Dr. Ruth's method, regardless of how long it appears to take. With that being said, let's free up our table for the next customer. I will definitely call you before we meet next month for lunch."

Barbara and Rose hugged as they exited the café to go their separate way.

*****

"Why are you up so early on a Friday?" Rose asked Janice.

"I am going into the clinic earlier to cover for someone. I should be finish at my usual time."

"Okay. Enjoy your day!" Rose shouted as she ran out the back door for her early morning jog with Josey.

*****

Janice had arrived ten minutes before her scheduled appointment with Dr. Ruth.

"How are you feeling?" Dr. Ruth asked Janice after handing her a bottle of water.

"I am feeling well. I felt emotionally drained when I left your office last week. The way I felt gave me insight as to why my mom was looking sad leaving your office last week. However, as you can see, it did not deter me from returning. My mom and I talked about facing the hard truth in order to heal before coming to you. I am here to do the work."

"That's good to hear. It can be uncomfortable talking about horrific events in your life. As you progress in the sessions, you will learn that the tragedy of these events has become your rock. These events do not define who you are, but you define them through your strength to act on your belief in a higher source, regardless of your circumstances. Let's start where we left off. Tell me about your state of being when your father died two weeks after your sixth birthday. In the mind of your six-year-old self, what was your thoughts on death? Were you angry at anyone?"

"Well, my six-year-old mind understood from Sunday school that death is a part of life. Although I did not understand much about death, I knew that when a person died, they would go to heaven. In Sunday school, I was taught to pray every night. The prayer I was taught to say is 'Now I lay me down to sleep, I pray the Lord my soul to keep. And if I died before I wake, I pray the Lord my soul to take.' As a child, I thought when a person gets in bed to sleep, they could die and not wake up. Also, in Sunday school, I was taught to say every morning, 'Thank you, God, for waking me up this morning.'

"When my mom told me and my brother that our dad had died in the hospital, I asked her how they knew he was dead and not asleep. I told Mom that every morning, we wake up from our sleep, we thank God for not being dead. But every day in the hospital, Dad was asleep. That was why JJ and I couldn't go see him. So how did they know Dad was not sleep again? Mom said because Dad stopped breathing in his sleep. I asked Mom if the Lord took his soul. Mom said yes. My thoughts on death at the age of six is that you go to sleep and stop breathing."

"In your last session, you made a statement and I quote, 'My dad was in the hospital two weeks when he died of complications from injuries due to the car accident.' Was this statement derived from your current state of mind on death?"

"Yes. However, I did not understand, until the age of thirteen, that people could die for many different causes; and that going to sleep is a metaphor to describe death. I think not having a clear understanding of death at the age of six is what prevented me from becoming angry at anyone at that particular time of my life. Once my understanding was broadened, I became angry. I was angry at God for not saving my dad's life. I was angry at my mom for not allowing me and JJ to go see our dad in the hospital. And I was angry at my dad for drinking and driving."

"Let's talk about your anger with your mom."

"Well, at age thirteen, I asked Mom why she didn't allow me and JJ to go see our dad in the hospital. She explained it was for JJ's and my protection. She said that exposing us to the horrific tragedy of Dad's injuries due to the accident would have been traumatizing. Mom explained this was the reason Dad had a closed casket at the funeral service. I now understand, but it took a long time for me to forgive my mom."

"When did you forgive your mom?"

"It was shortly after she divorced my stepfather, Craig, which was approximately four years ago."

"What change occurred that caused you to forgive her?"

"I don't know. I wasn't angry anymore. Thinking back, the only thing I can grasp from me forgiving Mom is time. Time heals all wounds, right?"

"It's possible your forgiveness has nothing to do with time healing the wound of anger. Are you still angry with God and your dad?"

"I don't think I am. I don't think about it. I know that God has the power to do the impossible. I know that he hears our prayers, and through faith, he answers them. I don't believe my dad had anyone praying for him. For this reason, there was no prayer for God to answer on behalf of my dad. It's not God's fault that no one prayed for my dad's life to be saved. For some reason, my understanding began to flourish at the age of thirteen. I realized praying the prayers learned in Sunday school wasn't my only option. I learned that I could pray to God about whatever is pressed upon my heart."

"What happened in your life that caused you to suddenly realize praying is broader than what you learned in Sunday school?"

"At age thirteen, I started attending church in the main sanctuary with Mom. I was too old for Sunday school in the children's church. The preacher's sermons helped me see things differently from Sunday school teaching."

"What caused you to no longer be angry with your dad?"

"For years, I was angry at Dad for drinking and driving. The preacher said in one of his sermons that when we allow life's circumstances to disconnect us from God, it opens the door for the influence of the adversary. He said either we are going to follow God or follow the adversary. My dad allowed the circumstance of my mom marrying Craig caused him to disconnect from God. Therefore, he was opened up to the influence of the adversary. My dad needed help. No one was there to help him."

"Janice, our time is up. I would love to explore this week's topic further in our next session."

Janice thanked Dr. Ruth as she stood to gather her things. Dr. Ruth escorted Janice out so she could call Rose in her office. Janice smiled as she passed her mom. She kissed her mom on the cheek as she passed through. Rose smiled then returned the kiss.

Rose greeted Dr. Ruth as she took her seat. She expressed how well Janice seemed to be adjusting to the change in their session time.

"Yes, the switch allows Janice to open up with clear focus and dialogue on her session rather than waver in her thoughts because her concerns are elsewhere," replied Dr. Ruth.

Rose noticed a small serving table added to the counseling office. On the table was a Keurig with an assorted supply of coffee and tea K-pods. There was a variety of sugar and cream with two sizes of coffee cups and lids. Dr. Ruth offered Rose a cup of coffee or tea. Rose gladly accepted a cup of caffeinated coffee with cream and one Equal sugar packet. Once Rose was settled with coffee in hand, Dr. Ruth asked Rose to talk about her divorce from James Sr.

"James serving me with divorce papers during my pregnancy was devastating. I questioned myself about so many things in my life, trying to figure out what went wrong. My emotions were all over the place. I wondered if James really loved me when we got married. I thought maybe he confused lust with love."

"What made you wonder if he lusted you rather than loved you?"

"I say this because the problem in our marriage started after JJ was born, and I was too tired to keep up with our sexual intimacy. Our intimacy went from four times or more a week to once a week. James constantly complained about the lack of sexual intimacy. He refused to acknowledge the increase in my workload. He had no interest in understanding what I was going through. When I realized our marriage was in trouble, I asked James if he would allow our pastor to counsel us. James's reply was, 'No man is going to tell me how to live my life. I am not a little boy who needs to run to some-one on how to be a man.' James was missing the point I was making, and he totally disregarded any discussion as I tried to bring clarity to my thoughts. James felt that, as a woman, I was programmed to be superhuman. James would often say God created woman from the rib bone of a man, whereas he created man from the dust of the ground. He felt God gave woman strength to bear the responsibilities of working in and out the home, cooking, cleaning, and taking care of the kids without lacking in giving her husband sexual intimacy. He felt the man's role is to have dominion over his wife, household, and to work. James felt when God told the woman in Genesis 3:16 of the Bible, 'Thy desire shall be to thy husband, and he shall rule over thee,' he was talking about sexual intimacy."

"What does the scripture mean to you?"

"I believe the entire scripture is God's reprimand to the woman for dishonoring the command told to her from Adam. This is the first command God gave to man in Genesis 2:16–17, which is to not eat from the tree of the knowledge of good and evil. Woman dishonor her husband by honoring the serpent. When man ate of the fruit from the forbidden tree that the woman gave to him, he dishonored God. Man's reprimand is shown in Genesis 3:22–24. I believe the scripture is telling woman that her desire shall be to honor her husband as he guides with godly commands by not allow-ing the influence of the adversary to cause her to dishonor him. Also, I believe the scripture tells man to not allow the influence of his wife to cause him to dishonor God's commandments."

"Rose, it's understandable your emotions were all over the place during your pregnancy. It is a scientific fact that pregnancy affects emotions due to the higher levels of both estrogen and progesterone. However, just because the emotion causes moments of sadness and anxiety doesn't mean you cannot trust your perceptions on life's circumstances, especially when you are using godly principles to guide you. The beautiful thing about Christ is that his sacrifice allows us as individuals to go behind the veil directly to God. Do you feel going directly to God for understanding that godly principles is dishonoring your husband?"

"No, Dr. Ruth, I do not. However, James had a way of making me feel guilty when I do not believe his interpretation of the scripture."

"You should not feel guilty for seeking God's guidance for understanding when your husband's perception of the scripture complexes or vexes your spirit. You are not, at that moment, seeking to hear and obey the voice of the adversary.

"What made you agree to the divorce by signing the papers?"

"I thought about all the times James cheated on me with different women and the effect of unsafe sexual intimacy with James due to his multiple partners. I thought about the unhealthiness of my emotional state in my pregnancy and as a mother to JJ. My desire to provide a mentally healthy, stable home for my kids outruled my desire to hold on to a man who doesn't want me or the child I was carrying. After the divorce was finalized, I put all my focus on my kids and healing from the loss. I gave in to whatever James's commands were in the divorce."

"What were James's commands?"

"James agreed to pay child support for JJ. He only agreed to pay child support for Janice after a paternity test confirmed he is the father. He asked for weekend visitations with JJ at his home. He asked that I waive my rights to spousal support. He asked to keep our home. After the divorce, I moved into a two-bedroom apartment with my newborn daughter and my son. When I was married to James, I was taking night classes at the local community college and later at the state university. After obtaining an associate of arts degree in business accounting and a bachelor's degree in business management, I continued to work as a paralegal because I wasn't ready to make a change in career. I didn't feel I was psychologically ready to give my thoughts to something new."

"How long were you single before meeting and marrying your second husband? But let's save this question for our next session. Our time is up."

Rose expressed to Dr. Ruth how her comments helped her let go of guilt she had carried pertaining to the failure of her first marriage. As Rose exited, she turned back around, smiled, and told Dr. Ruth to have a pleasant weekend.

Rose was so inspired by her last counseling session with Dr. Ruth that she decided to start a nonprofit organization to help unwed moms. That evening, Rose shared her plans about the nonprofit with Janice. Janice was so intrigued, and she offered to help her mom. Janice suggested that they go to the family lake house for the weekend to plan.

"I like the way you think," replied Rose with a smile.

Rose and Janice woke up early on Saturday morning preparing for the lake house. As Janice loaded the car with their overnight bags and groceries, Rose gathered Josey's bed, food, toys, and favorite treats. Two and half hours after merging on the highway, they arrived at the lake house. They took a moment to put things away and prepared a light breakfast. Josey was very familiar with the gated wood area, so Rose let her out to run around.

After cleaning the breakfast dishes, Rose and Janice grabbed their laptops and met in the lounge area out back. The both sat near each other in matching chaise lounge chairs with a small round table between the chairs. They adjusted the back of their chairs to sit upright. After taking a moment to enjoy the view of the lake while enjoying the serenity of nature, Janice asked her mom if she had a name for the nonprofit.

"I have two. I would like for us to choose one of the two names. The first name is Sarah's Daughters. The second name is Iron Sharping Iron Women's Empowerment."

Janice asked her mom the meaning behind her choosing each of those names.

"I feel each woman can relate in some way to Sarah, wife of Abraham. Sarah was childless and barren when God promised Abraham to bless her with child and make her a mother of nations [Gen. 17:15–16]. When Sarah heard Abraham laughed at God's promise to bless her with a son [Gen. 17:17], Sarah laughed as well [Gen. 18:12]. Sarah's life revolved around pleasing her husband and following his command. There is nothing wrong with her wanting to please her husband; however, she allowed her circumstances to misguide her method in pleasing Abraham. Because she was unable to have children, she gave her handmaid to Abraham to have a child for her. At age ninety, God's promise to Sarah was fulfilled. Sarah conceived a child with her husband. From her lineage came Isaac, her son, and King David, from which came the Savior.

"Many women find that their life has centered around pleasing a man and following his commands, which can be with fault at times, such as lying for him [Gen. 12:11–13]. When this man is no longer in their life, the woman feel lost, without purpose or direction. Our mission is to help these daughters of Sarah find their purpose and provide aid to them in a holistic way.

"As you can see, a detailed explanation had to be given to provide the concept of the name Sarah's Daughters; however, the name Iron Sharping Iron Women's Empowerment can be self-explanatory for many women. The name itself states our mission: to strengthen one another through positive encouraging, coaching, care, and developing with clear and honest conversations. In Proverbs 27:17, the Bible declares, 'Iron sharpeneth iron; so, a man sharpeneth the countenance of his friend.' Part of our mission would be to offer moral support in the enhancement of our sisters' emotions, mood, character, and mental composure."

"Mom, I like both these names and the meaning behind them. As a suggestion, I think we should name the nonprofit Iron Sharping Iron Women's Empowerment and add the concept of Sarah's Daughters into the mission statement."

"Good idea, Janice. I agree with your suggestion. I would love for this to become a family project. Next weekend, on Sunday, at our family dinner, I would like to get the family input and see if they would become a board member. We will need at least five to seven board members to qualify and function as a 501(c)(3). Let's change clothes and go for a light jog around the lake before lunch. After lunch, we can meet here again to discuss the type of service we will provide, and based on the name and service, we can put together our mission statement."

"Sounds good, Mom."

*****

After a pleasant weekend at the lake house, Janice awakened on Monday morning energetic and excited to face the last week of interning. She was ready to find a permanent job as a physical therapist. Rose wished Janice well as she headed out the door earlier than usual to prepare for her staff meeting. She decided to pick up bagels and donuts for the meeting. She needed to meet with her business partner before the 9:00-a.m. meeting to go over the promotion of their top salesperson and the awards of recognition for many of the salespersons.

Midday, Rose received a text from Janice. She was excited that the clinic offered her a permanent position with a very good salary and was eager to tell someone that she accepted a permanent position at the clinic. Rose briefly congratulated Janice in a reply text with a lot of emojis expressing her excitement for her.

At home, Rose asked Janice how her new permanent work hours would work with her weekly counseling sessions. Janice informed Rose her schedule would remain the same. She would work nine hours on Mondays through Thursdays and four hours on Fridays.

*****

"It's good to see you, Janice. You look well. You have a glow. Do you care to share what the glow is about?" asked Dr. Ruth.

"Yes. I am now a professional licensed physical therapist, and I am working for the same clinic where I completed my internship."

"Congratulations, Janice. It's good to hear and see the excitement of your accomplishment. I know you will do well because of your compassionate, patient personality. Physical therapy is an excellent field for you to work. Do you need a minute before we get started?"

"No," replied Janice. "I'm ready to dive in."

"You ended our last session with a very powerful statement. I would like for you to elaborate on your statement, 'My dad needed help. No one was there to help him.' What does this mean?"

"Looking back at what I know about my dad and his family issues with his siblings, I can see how he could have felt alone, because he *was* alone. My mom was his only caring family when they were married. He went to church because my mom went to church. I don't believe my dad had a relationship with God."

"What is having a relationship with God to you?"

"Having a relationship with God in my perspective is reading your Bible, conversing with God in daily prayers, finding a quiet time to meditate on God's Word, and in this quiet time, talk to God about problems or thoughts. I believe my mom was too emotionally hurt and angry at my dad to pray for him in the way he needed prayer. My dad was not an active member in the church, where he could have called a church member to ask for prayer. My mom said my dad believed in God, but he did not go to church as a child. His belief came from his grandmother reading Bible stories to him. His mom was violated as a teen by a church member and never returned to church. My dad's only living family members during his marriage to my mom were his older sister, an older brother, and a younger brother. My dad was the responsible one of his siblings. Dad would talk to JJ about his siblings during his weekend visits after having a couple glasses of wine. JJ shared what Dad told him with me. My mom knows the issues my dad had with his siblings, but she has no knowledge that JJ and I know.

"As a teen, my dad worked odd jobs to help his mom after his dad died. He worked his way through law school. When his mom became ill, he took care of her while working a full-time job. He moved his mom into his home with the assistance of a day nurse while he worked. His siblings expressed it was my dad's responsibility to take care for their mother because he was the only single child and did not have the responsibility of taking care of a family.

"My dad was very distraught when his mother died. His siblings appeared to be stronger than him and offered to help with the funeral arrangement. My dad gave his younger brother the key to their mom's storage to check for her life insurance policy and banking information. He assigned the obituary to his sister, but his older brother asked to handle the task. He reassigned his sister the task of purchasing proper attire and a wig for their mom. My dad found a mortuary to pick up his mom's body and promised to return with her insurance papers. His younger brother claimed their mom did not have an insurance policy or a bank account. He claimed the paperwork in storage was just junk mail. My dad asked for the return of the storage key so he could look. My dad recalled his mother telling him that he was the beneficiary of her life insurance policy. He was surprised when his brother couldn't find a policy or a bank statement. Dad knew his mother received monthly direct deposit from Social Security. He never used her money or thought to check her bank account each month while she was in his care. He remembered putting her debit card and bank papers in a large envelope and putting it in storage with her other belongings. He felt it would be okay since he had the only key. Within his mind, Dad questioned his brother but did not have the energy to verbalize his thoughts. Dad's priorities were getting his mom's funeral arrangements taken care of without family disputes.

"Dad decided to pay for the service out of pocket. Approximately one month after my grandmother's funeral service, Dad decided to take a couple of days off work to go through his mother's belongings. He donated her furniture and clothing to shelters. He couldn't understand why only junk mail was in the storage when he knew other important documents were placed in there by him. Dad recalled seeing a P.O. Box number on the important documents he placed in storage. He looked up the address of the local post office. With a copy of his mother's dead certificate in hand, Dad went to the post office to request access to his mother's box. Dad gained access to his mother's postal box after providing additional information about his mom. With a bag full of mail to sort through, Dad found his mother's bank statement and immediately made calls to stop all recurring deductions from her account. One of the deductions was for life insurance. He contacted the insurance company, explaining that he did not know the policy number but had his mom's social security number. After the insurance rep identified Dad as James Jackson, the beneficiary, the insurance representative informed Dad that an alert was placed on the account because of possible fraud. Per the representative, someone called in stating the beneficiary name on the policy was a typo. The caller stated the actual name should be John Jackson instead of James Jackson. Also, the representative stated the caller never returned the documents requested or mailed. The representative confirmed documents were mailed to Dad's younger brother's, John Jackson, address.

"When Dad gathered his siblings together to confront his brother John, to his surprise, JoAnn, Dad's sister, confessed to the fraud plot among all three siblings. My dad's siblings told him they felt the money should go where it was needed most among them three. They had no remorse for their actions to steal death benefits. Dad never communicated with his siblings again after their confession to him.

"Outside of JJ and myself, my dad had no close family or friends. My dad needed help to get through his life problems. Looking back, I feel my dad self-medicated with alcoholic drinks. No one was there to see he needed help. My dad pushed my mom away, then became angry when she married someone else. Because my mom is the reason my dad went to church and had some type of stable family life, when Dad separated from Mom, he also separated himself from God; however, Mom didn't separate herself from God. Of course, she was angry at my dad for divorcing her, but she should have prayed for him."

"In your first session with me, you talked about overhearing a conversation between your mom and dad when you were around four or five. You heard your dad tell your mom that she should be happy he was paying child support for a child he did not want. Also, you talked about how your brother blamed you for the absence of your father when your mom demanded him to come in the house to see you. How did you feel about what your dad and brother said?"

"I did not want my dad or my brother to be angry with me. I blamed myself for Dad not seeing JJ. I blamed myself for Dad divorcing Mom because I was born."

"Janice, it's normal for kids to blame themselves for their parents' anger or disappointments in life. Sometimes parents say things that sound ill-hearted when they are angry. Anger blinds a person from expressing themselves in a rational manner. Anger is a form of emotional hurt, and hurt people hurt other people. So when your dad said the ill-hearted things to your mom, he was trying to hurt her because he was hurting. I think you and your mom need to have a conversation regarding her praying for your dad after his accident. Sometimes it's difficult for a wounded person to pray for the person who wounded them, but it doesn't stop the wounded person from asking others to pray for the person who has wounded them. Assumption without confirmation causes one to hold on to a false perception of the truth, which, in turn, can cause resentment.

"Our session for this week has come to an end. Next week, I would like to allow time for you to ask any questions or express any concerns about what we talked about thus far. Also, we can talk about your relationship with your stepdad, Craig, if time permits."

"Thanks, Dr. Ruth. I will see you next week."

Dr. Ruth made a note in her laptop to have her secretary email Rose and Janice, expressing her discussion in delaying their group session until further notice. She felt the focus was most needed in their individual sessions before coming together for a family session. Then Dr. Ruth escorted Rose into her office.

"Hello, Rose. How are you feeling?"

"I am well, Dr. Ruth. It has been a long week."

"Anything you care to discuss in this week's session?"

"Well, it's nothing that warrants counseling. I'm starting a non-profit for unwed moms."

"What inspired you to start a nonprofit?" asked Dr. Ruth.

"I was inspired after our last counseling session. Discussing my divorce from James caused me to reflect on how alone I felt becoming a single mom with two young kids. I'm grateful I had my full-time job as a paralegal and child support to help. Nevertheless, I was financially burdened due to childcare. It took a long time before I could financially move into a larger place. Janice was almost four when I rented a small three-bedroom house. I didn't know where to seek resources that aid in finding reasonable childcare programs. I was psychologically drained and felt as if I needed someone with a clear mind to think for me. The nonprofit will be a one-stop resource center that caters to the unwed mother's various needs."

"Rose, I have several colleagues in the medical field who would love to donate time and money toward the welfare of the unwed moms. Let's talk again after you are up and running. In the meantime, I will put together a list of medical professionals who currently assist pro bono.

"Let's start where we left off last week. We ended with me asking you a question. How long were you single before meeting and marrying your second husband?"

"Dr. Ruth, I was single long before my divorce from James was final. I was divorced over four years when I met Craig. Craig and I met at JJ's tenth birthday party. Craig is the cousin of my best friend, Barbara. He came to JJ's birthday party with his ten-year-old nephew. Because the party was hosted at Barbara's house, I asked her to invite her family members with their kids. At the party, Craig introduced himself and thanked me for allowing him and his nephew to share in the festivities. Craig and I spent the entire party talking to each other. He is a friendly, kind-hearted man who loves to talk. He is totally opposite to James in looks. He isn't tall, dark, muscularly built, or handsome. Craig is five feet eight inches tall with a medium-size pot belly and facial blemishes. The warmth and gentleness of his spirit is what drew me to him.

"Craig owned several autobody shops. He had never been married but was engaged once. His family and friends finally convinced him that his fiancé was using him for his money. She had four kids and a boyfriend on the side. Craig was mesmerized by her beauty. It wasn't until her boyfriend confronted Craig that he realized she did not love him.

"Craig called me every day after JJ's party. He never missed a day. Each day, we would talk at least thirty minutes on the phone, sometimes more. I never had this type of relationship with a man. I did not know any man this caring or compassionate. There wasn't anything that we couldn't talk about. Eight months after meeting Craig, we were having dinner at one of my favorite restaurants when he asked me to marry him. I was frozen and couldn't speak. Craig asked me if I was okay. I told him I didn't see the question of marriage coming and needed time to digest what he had asked me. Unlike James, Craig was a spiritual man who went to church at least two Sundays a month and Bible study every Wednesday evening. After taking a week to pray and meditate on Craig's proposal, I could see clearly how easy it was to say yes to James and question if Craig was the right person for me. I was attracted to James for all the wrong reasons. I was attracted to his looks, his height, his charm, and his profession. James was not a communicator with me. We would sit and watch TV together without engaging in conservation with each other. We would go out to dinner on a date and talk only 10 percent of the time while we are waiting on the food to be served. Once the food comes, the conversation stops. Our conversations were about work. After JJ was born, our conversations were arguing about what I wasn't doing for him as a wife. I kept asking myself why I loved this man. So in my quiet time, I asked myself why I am questioning if Craig was the right person. He is considerate of my feelings, time, kids, and all that matters to me. He listens and responds in conversation. He opens doors for me. He pulls out my chair before I sit. He carries heavy things for me. He is handy around the house. For all these reasons and more, I told Craig yes two weeks after his marriage proposal to me.

"Craig wanted to elope with me and the kids to Las Vegas. He did not want the naysayers to have a say in our decision. Nine months after meeting Craig, we were married in a private Las Vegas ceremony with only the kids in attendance. We later had a party to commence our marriage with family and friends."

"Rose, how did the kids feel about you marrying Craig?"

"JJ was excited about having Craig join the family. Four months after I married Craig, JJ told me he had a dream that Craig would ask me to marry him. In his dream, James Sr. told JJ that it was okay for his mom to marry Craig. That Craig would be a good addition to the family, and he would spend a lot of time with him. James asked JJ to be patient with Janice because she was still healing emotionally. He told JJ that I would have a child with Craig. I was extremely surprised when JJ shared his dream with me months later. As a kid, JJ was very much like his dad, a person who communicated very little. I told JJ that God speaks to us in many different ways, and God was using his dad's image to talk to him in his dream."

"Rose, what made you tell JJ it was God who was talking to him in his dream?"

"Because JJ told me about the dream right after I made a doctor's appointment to see if I was pregnant. The appointment was made earlier in the day at work, and JJ told me that evening after dinner. I did not mention to anyone about the appointment.

"The comment JJ made about Janice was true. She did not receive Craig into the family the way JJ had. I believe too many emotional changes occurred to Janice soon after her dad came into her life. She met her dad for the first time at JJ's tenth birthday party. He embraced her after seeing how much she looks like his mother. Her dad not only came but planned her fifth birthday party. She finally started to spend time with her dad, which was short-lived. A year and three months after spending time with her dad, he dies. Less than a year after her father died, I was marrying Craig and was expecting another child. Chloe was born seven months after Janice's seventh birthday. Chloe's dad was present for her birth and was excited about welcoming his only child into the world." Rose then began to cry.

Dr. Ruth handed Rose some tissue and gave her a moment to release the emotion with her tears. "Rose, I need you to put this emotional breakthrough into words so that it loses hold on you."

"I never thought this depth about what Janice went through as a kid without her father, and when he finally came into her life, all these emotional changes took place. I feel guilty for not seeing it sooner and for being a contributor. How could I not allow my child time to heal before I added more to her plate? What kind of mother am I to not see what I was putting my child through?"

"You have to remember, Rose, you and Janice were in the same place. You were too wounded to naturally see Janice's wounds. Spiritually, you were in tune with Janice. This is why she is spiritually strong. You gave her what she needed spiritually to stand against the fiery darts of the wicked, even if it was your darts the adversary was using. From a child up, you taught Janice how to put on the whole armor of God that she may be able to stand and not crash."

"Thank you, Dr. Ruth. I needed to hear this and see Janice emotional wounds."

"Let's end this week's session here. Next week, I would like for you to talk more about your marriage to Craig."

*****

Saturday morning, after jogging with Josey, Rose showered and surprised Janice with her favorite breakfast. Rose prepared fresh strawberry crepes, hash browns with over-easy eggs, and turkey bacon. She squeezed fresh orange juice. During breakfast, they discussed the plans for their family dinner on Sunday. After breakfast, Rose called JJ and his wife, Grace, as well as Chloe and her husband, Robert, to coordinate the family dinner plans. JJ and Robert agreed to bring meat for the grill. Chloe and Grace were responsible for preparing side dishes. Janice made a list of drinks to purchase before heading out the door to run errands. Rose called the farmer's market bakery to place a pickup order. She ordered a dozen assortment of cupcakes and a dozen assortment of mini cheesecakes. The pickup order would be ready in three hours, giving Rose time to review her notes on the nonprofit. Then the phone rang. It was her best friend, Barbara.

"Hi, Barbara. How are things going?" asked Rose.

"All is well with me, Rose. I'm calling to check on my little cousin to see how she is holding up with the news regarding her grandmother's surgery that has been scheduled for next week."

"What do you mean, Barbara? Chloe did not mention anything to me this morning when I talked to her about Mother Baker being sick."

"Well, it's possible she doesn't know yet. Her dad, Craig, will be driving into town on Tuesday to be present for his mom's hip replacement surgery on Wednesday. I found out this morning from my brother. I haven't talked to Craig. Well, you know the story. He doesn't talk to me after he and you divorced because of our friendship. He has to understand you and I have been friends long before he came into the picture, and we are not going to stop being friends because he and you are no longer a couple. I will text you the name and address of the hospital so you can pass it on to Chloe. I don't want to take up much of your time. I know this is the weekend you and the kids come together for family dinner. I hope you all enjoy your day together, and do not allow this news to put a damper on the festivities. When a person transitions to be with the Lord, we call it a homegoing celebration. Aunt Cassie Baker is still with us in the flesh, so enjoy the celebration of unity among family at tomorrow's dinner."

"Thank you, Barbara, for thinking of Chloe. I will make sure she is informed. I appreciate and love you. I will talk with you later."

Just as Rose ended her call with Barbara, her phone rang. It was Chloe calling. Rose was prepared in her mind to cancel the family dinner tomorrow if Chloe wasn't up to it.

"Hi, Mom. Do you have a minute?"

"Yes, Chloe. I have all the time you need."

"I am calling to let you know that Grandmother is ill. She is in the hospital and is scheduled to have surgery next week. I just finish talking to Dad on the phone. He will be back in town on Tuesday."

"Chloe, I just ended a phone conversation with Barbara. She called to make sure you were informed and was okay. How are you holding up?"

"I'm okay, Mom. I am more concerned about Grandmother Cassie and her age, as well as Dad, than myself. Dad did not sound well. Although he knows his mom, at the age of ninety, has lived a long prosperous life, he still isn't ready to accept the possibility of losing her to death. I prayed with Dad before ending our phone conversation. All I can do now is trust God. Mom, I know how considerate and passionate you are as a person, so I am letting you know I am okay. Please do not cancel tomorrow's family dinner. We need to celebrate life, not mourn death. I need to see my family right now laughing and having fun, basically enjoying each other's company."

"You know me well, Chloe. I was prepared to cancel the family dinner. We will continue with our plans. I am looking forward to spending quality time with you all. Please know we are all here for you. I have an hour before I pick up my bakery order. Call me if you need me."

"Okay, Mom. Will do."

After Rose hang up the phone, she read a few scriptures from her Bible before praying for Mother Baker, Chloe, and Craig. She ran out to pick up her bakery. She called JJ while in her car to share the conversation she had with Chloe. JJ reiterated what his mom told Chloe. He ended the call saying, 'We are here to support Chloe in whatever capacity is needed.' Janice was on one accord with the family when Rose told her about the conversation with Chloe.

"Mom, the theme of tomorrow's dinner should be celebrating life."

"Janice, I concur."

*****

JJ and Chloe arrived as scheduled, around noon, with their families for a small lunch. Rose had prepared buffalo wings with dipping sauce and a veggie tray. Trey was served a peanut butter and jelly sandwich with a sliced apple for lunch. For dinner, Chloe prepared broccoli salad with raisins and walnuts. She bought corn on the cob for the grill. Grace prepared potato salad, as well as a fruit salad. JJ bought washed and seasoned chicken quarters to put on the grill. Robert bought salmon and beef shish kebobs for the grill.

After the family greeted Chloe with love offerings of support, JJ prayed for Chloe, Craig, and Mother Cassie Baker, as well as blessing the food. As the family ate lunch, Rose read the initial meeting notes on the role and responsibility of the nonprofit board members, as well as the bylaws.

"As you all know, the name of the nonprofit is Iron Sharping Iron Women's Empowerment. The mission of the nonprofit is to promote the self-actualization of women so they are able to find meaning and purpose in life as a woman. The purpose of the nonprofit is to help women with educational resources, childcare resources, financial resources, mental and psychological resource, as well as legal resources. I have a list of professionals who are willing to donate time in every aspect of the care we will provide to women. Also, I have a list of other nonprofits who are willing to partner with us in providing specific resources, such as housing, childcare, transportation, etc. Right now, I need each board member to review the bylaws and finalize your acceptance with a signature. Once the bylaws are signed, we can submit the 501(c)(3) application to the secretary of state. The confirmed board members are myself, serving in the capacity of chair and president; JJ, serving in the capacity of vice-chair; Chloe, serving in the capacity of secretary; Robert and Janice, serving in the capacity as board members; and Grace, serving in the capacity as board member and treasurer. Please acknowledge your acceptance by signing the bylaws."

After signing the bylaws, JJ asked Robert if he was ready to start the grill. The ladies set up the patio lounge area for a game of Charades. Trey rode his tricycle and played with Legos as the adults enjoyed themselves playing games and telling old stories. After dinner, the ladies cleaned the kitchen while JJ and Robert cleaned the grill. The remaining food was placed in to-go containers. Before calling it a night, they all gathered in the family room for dessert.

*****

Rose took off work on Wednesday to be with Chloe at the hospital. Although she and Craig did not divorce on bad terms, it felt awkward seeing him again. Rose hugged Craig upon sight. She expressed her sorrow for his mom and let him know that Mother Baker was in her prayers. Craig thanked Rose for her support and prayers.

Craig and Chloe went into Mother Baker's room as other family and friends waited in the guest waiting room. Thirty minutes later, Craig and Chloe joined everyone in the guest waiting room. They reported that Mother Baker was being transported to the operating room, and the doctors would come talk to them after she came out of surgery. Chloe sat holding her dad's hand while others read books, played on their cell phones, or engaged in conversation with each other. Rose, sitting apart from Chloe and Craig, was reading a book when Craig's older cousin Ralph approached her. He asked Rose why was she at the hospital. Rose let him know she was there to support Chloe and Craig. Ralph stared long and hard at Rose before telling her that she was no longer a family member and suggested that she could support Chloe and Craig from home or any other place than at the hospital. Rose smelled alcohol on Ralph as he talked.

"Look at you sitting here with your high-and-mighty self, acting like you care."

In a soft voice, Rose told Ralph it was not the time or place for that type of behavior from him. Craig overheard his cousin and immediately jumped up to defend Rose.

"Ralph!" Craig shouted. "Please, for God's sake, leave Rose alone. We are all here for the same purpose, and this is not the time for you to confront her on how you feel life should have turned out. You will respect my ex-wife of twenty years and the mother of my only child. If you are finding it difficult to do so, then you leave because Rose is not going anywhere."

Chloe came over and hugged her mom. She grabbed Rose by the hand and escorted her to the chair next to where she sat with her dad. Ralph frowned as he left the guest room. Others in the room shook their heads in disbelief.

Three hours later, two doctors entered the guest room. They approached Craig and Chloe to let them know that Mother Baker's surgery went well. The doctors suggested they go have lunch because Mother Baker would be in recovery for about an hour, and they would not be able to visit with her until she was back in her room.

Craig offered to take Chloe and Rose to lunch. Rose declined, but Chloe asked her mom to please come with them to lunch. Rose accepted the offer. They walked to a local café next door to the hospital. As always, Craig was the perfect gentleman. He opened the door for Rose and Chloe. He pulled out their chairs and paid for the meal. Rose began to think about all the reasons she married Craig. To Rose's surprise, her conversation with Craig at lunch was pleasant. They laughed and joked like old times. She asked herself why she was surprised he would be someone other than who he had always been.

Craig thanked Rose and Chloe for helping him to take his mind off worrying about his mother. Craig further expressed how laughing really was good for the soul because it had shifted his thoughts from doom to hope, allowing him to feel optimistic about the outcome of his mother's surgery.

Heading back to the hospital, Chloe walked between her parents, holding each of their hands. She thought about how much she missed the good times they had as a family. She couldn't understand what happened to cause her parents to divorce. She always wanted to ask but was scared it would open wounds or prevent wounds from healing. She began to smile, thinking about fun memories of her family. Craig looked at Chloe and noticed she was in deep thought as they walk. Craig made the statement, "A penny for your thought," as Chloe began to smile. Chloe was startled by her dad's comment. It made her realize she was wearing her thoughts on her face again. She told her dad that she was thinking about a past event.

Mother Baker was in her room when they arrived back at the hospital. Rose went to the waiting room as Craig and Chloe visited with Mother Baker. An hour later, Craig and Chloe returned to the waiting room to provide an update on Mother Baker to family and friends. Craig expressed his gratitude to everyone for coming to the hospital to support him and Chloe. He thanked them for their prayers and well-wishes. He informed everyone that at that moment, his mother was recovering well. She was alert yet very drowsy from the anesthesia. He further expressed that, according to the doctors, she would be heavily sedated for the next couple of days, and he would keep them all up-to-date on her recovery progress. He asked that they all go home to their families and to continue to keep them in their prayers. He informed them that he would be sleeping on a cot at the hospital in his mother's room.

Everyone gathered their things to leave. Each person hugged Craig and Chloe as they exited. Rose was the last to leave. She offered to bring Craig home-cooked meals to the hospital as he stayed with his mom. Craig thanked Rose but declined. He kissed her on the cheek as she exited the room. Chloe kissed her mom as well.

*****

"I cannot believe Friday is here already," Janice commented to Rose as she headed out the door for work.

"Yes. This week passed swiftly. Have a good day. I will see you later," replied Rose.

*****

"Good afternoon, Dr. Ruth."

"Hello, Janice. How are you?"

"I am well, Dr. Ruth."

As Janice settled with her drink, Dr. Ruth briefly read, in silence, through the last note she made from last week's session with Janice.

"Janice, we ended last week's session with me expressing that I would like to allow you time to ask questions or express concerns from our previous sessions. Do you have any questions or concerns you would like to address?"

"I took your advice in the last session. I had a conversation with my mom in regards to praying for Dad. I asked Mom if she ever prayed for someone who was hurting her or had caused her pain. From this question, my mom and I discussed her praying for my dad. Mom said it was very difficult for her to pray for Dad at the end of their marriage because she was emotionally distraught and drained. She would ask others to pray for her and dad. Mom said it took several months after the divorce to regain the emotional strength that allowed her to pray for Dad without being judgmental. Hearing this from Mom gave me peace. I now know people were praying for Dad, including my mom."

"Janice, I'm elated to hear you had a conversation with your mom, and you now have clarity regarding your dad not having anyone to pray for him. Let's talk about your relationship with Craig, your stepdad. How did you adjust to your mom marrying Craig shortly after your dad died?"

"Dr. Ruth, my mom marrying Craig was a very confusing and difficult time for my six-year-old self to digest and understand. In my mind, my dad divorced Mom because she was pregnant with me at a time when my dad did not want any more kids. At first, I could not understand why Mom and Dad did not remarry after Dad accepted me as his daughter. When Mom married Craig seven months after Dad's acceptance of me, I received understanding. Craig is the reason my dad and mom did not remarry each other. He is the reason my family could not get back together, and he is the reason for my dad's drinking. I believed Dad started drinking because he was angry Mom married someone else. I love my little sister, Chloe. I watched my sister experience the life I could only dream of experiencing. And I blamed Craig for taking away my experience. Craig was at the hospital with Mom when Chloe was born. My dad was not at the hospital when I was born. He did not see me until I was five years old. Craig had a party for his firstborn child when Chloe was six months old. No one celebrated my birth. Craig spoiled Chloe and took her many places. My dad did not take me anywhere before the age of five. Although Chloe and I have a healthy close relationship, I envy the relationship she has with her dad. I always felt left out."

"Janice, I see you presently hold Craig responsible for you not experiencing the dynamics of family in the way Chloe has experienced family. Let's look at this in steps. Your dad served your mom with divorce papers when she was pregnant with you. Your mom, JJ, and you lived as a family unit five years before meeting Craig and nearly six years before Craig joined the family. Your dad fell in love with you on sight when you were five. Your dad was sharing his family issues with JJ after having a couple of drinks, long before meeting you. After meeting you, your dad did not express his willingness to unite as a family. He continued as usual, with JJ coming to his home for a weekend visit. The only difference is he added you to the visits with JJ. Seeing this truth should help you to see that Craig is not responsible for the actions of your dad. Seeing this truth is not to shift your blame from Craig to your dad. Seeing this truth is to help you see the truth of your anger by removing the veil from your eyes. You have a legitimate reason for your hurt. You felt isolated and abandoned as a child due to the absence of your dad. It's difficult to heal from past hurt when you hide the truth. And it's okay to be angry at someone you love. But it is not okay to blame someone else for your anger because you don't want to blame the person you love. Take a minute to digest what I just said. Tell me what you are feeling."

Janice sat in silence for about two minutes with her eyes closed. Tears fell from her eyes. Dr. Ruth handed her some tissue.

"Dr. Ruth, I now see that envy of my sister's relationship with her father has caused me to blame him for the lack of relationship I wanted with my dad and mom as a married couple. I did not want Craig to be a perfect person in my eyes because I did not want envy to turn to jealousy. I wanted to continue to love my sister without feeling jealous of her having a caring father who was married to our mother and who spends time with her. So in my mind, I had to create Craig equal to my dad in blame. My dad divorced my mom and separated himself from his family. Blaming Craig for my dad's actions helped me to not like him more than my dad. In reality, Craig is the perfect father. Craig sharing the blame helped me to feel equal to my sister and Craig to be equal to my father. Because I could not find any imperfections in Craig's character, I made one up. Now I see. I spent years disliking Craig when I should have been enjoying the love he showed us all equally."

"Janice, this is a major breakthrough for you. It's not too late to enjoy family. Although your mom and Craig are now divorced, he did not divorce himself from you and your siblings. Adults still can enjoy the love and care of their parents. Craig helped in raising you. It's not too late to show your appreciation for the values he taught and the love he showed."

"Dr. Ruth, I concur."

"Good. Our session has come to an end. Have a pleasant weekend."

"You too, Dr. Ruth."

Dr. Ruth called Rose into her office. After Dr. Ruth and Rose greeted and settled, Dr. Ruth read the last note she made of Rose's last session out loud, "Let's start where you left off last week. Tell me about your marriage to Craig."

"My marriage to Craig was everything a person could have hoped for in a marriage. Craig was a good father, husband, and provider. As a father, Craig accepted and treated JJ and Janice as if they were his biological kids. When JJ asked to play basketball and little league football, Craig took him to enroll and was present at every practice and game. He would take JJ and his nephews on camping trips. Although JJ was extremely hurt when his father died, he immediately accepted Craig. As I had mentioned previously, JJ's acceptance of Craig came after a dream he had about his dad and him discussing Craig asking me to marry him. On the other hand, Janice was too emotionally hurt about her dad's death to accept Craig as her stepdad. I was concerned about Janice when I became pregnant with Chloe. I was concerned about her emotional stability. But to my surprise, she accepted Chloe well. Chloe was like a living baby doll to Janice. She wanted to comb her hair, bathe her, feed her, and dress her. But Janice did not want Craig to be close to Chloe. When Craig would try to spend time with the girls together, Janice would withdraw by isolating herself from the festivities. Janice would only participate if I was involved or if it was a family event. Craig understood Janice was hurting. Therefore, he allowed her to go at her pace, never pushing himself on her."

"What are your thoughts on why Janice did not want a close relationship with Craig? And did she ever, during the duration of your marriage to Craig, accept him as her stepfather?"

"I believe Janice did not accept Craig because she did not want the memories of her relationship with her dad to be replaced or to feel like she was betraying her dad. At family events, Janice would often talk about the time she had with her dad. Although her time with James was short-lived, she would repeat the events over and over again. Craig made sure he would give her his undivided attention when she talked about her dad. He would always thank her for sharing the fun events she shared with her dad. Janice was around fifteen when she stopped talking about her dad. Janice became an introvert in her late teens. She would spend time alone drawing, painting, and going to museums. Sometimes she and Chloe would go to the beach or museums together. Occasionally, she would hang out with friends from school. Although Janice was respectful toward Craig, she never became close to him. Janice changed to this bubbly person after Craig and I divorced. She immediately, at the age of twenty-six, moved back home after Craig and I divorced.

"As a husband, Craig was very affectionate. He loved holding hands in public. He loved having date nights. He would listen to my casual conversation with others and would surprise me with things I had expressed were on my wish list. Craig made sure his family was priority. He never put me second to his family or to his friends. Craig was a great provider. He worked hard. Although he had employed managers to run his body shops, he oversaw all operations, especially the financial side of his business. Overseeing three shops kept him busy but never too busy for his family."

"Rose, I haven't heard you say one ill thing about Craig. What caused you and him to divorce?"

"I don't really understand what happened to change my way of thinking. Suddenly, after twenty years, I woke up and realized the things that caused me to say yes to Craig's marriage proposal was no longer valid. It wasn't that he changed, it was I who changed. I expected Craig to do the things he did to the point that they did not excite me any longer. I expected him to open the door for me or pull out my chair before I sat. I expected him to be a good provider or surprise me with gifts. I expected him to carry heavy items or make minor repairs around the house. What I expected no longer brought me a feeling of joy or privilege."

"Rose, did you love Craig when you married him?"

"I don't know. I know that I loved him during our marriage."

"Do you know if you have ever been in love with Craig? I ask this question assuming you understand the difference between being in love with someone versus loving them."

"I understand the difference, Dr. Ruth. I was in love with James. Because I was in love with James, I accepted a lot of hurtful things from James. I made excuses for the pain he caused me. If James hadn't served me with divorce papers, I would have stayed in the relationship, accepting whatever hurtful things he was doing to me. I have never felt the type of love I had for James with anyone ever, including Craig. With this being said, no, I was never in love with Craig."

"Rose, let's revisit the first question I asked you. What caused you and Craig to divorce?"

Rose began to cry. "I divorced Craig because the love I have for him as a good father, provider, and husband is not enough to hold my interest when these things were depleting in quality within my thoughts. The kids are adults and have moved out the house. I have become a business owner, and I am providing for myself. I don't share the same romantic feelings that Craig shares for me. Although he is a good man, I am not in love with him."

"Rose, do you think you were protecting your feelings by not falling in love with Craig?"

"Dr. Ruth, I put up a wall of protection after James. I did not ever want to feel that level of hurt from anyone. I promised myself to never give another person that type of power and control over my emotions ever again. Unfortunately, the first man I fell in love with did not have the qualities that Craig have as a father, husband, and provider. And because of this hurtful experience with James, it damaged my way of thinking toward love. Dr. Ruth, I would have loved to experience the process of being in love with Craig. I often wondered if it is possible to be in love with someone who is a good person and who is equally in love with you. Every couple I know have problems in their relationship. Many are divorced now, and others are holding on to unhappy relationships. Craig and I never had any problems. I did not want to hold on to an unhappy marriage. What is wrong with me? Why couldn't I fall in love with Craig the way he loves me?"

"Rose, I think you know the answer. You just spoke it. You were guarding your heart and emotions after your experience with James."

"How do I change my way of thinking?"

"Rose, you are a spiritual lady. As you already know, all things are possible with God. It's time to take this issue to him."

"Thank you, Dr. Ruth, for allowing God to use you in this session. I never spent time with God about what I was feeling in my marriage with Craig. I now understand why the preacher would say even the preacher needs a preacher."

"Rose, I am happy for the breakthrough. I am looking forward to hearing about your communion with God. Take care, Rose. I will see you next week."

Rose hugged Dr. Ruth as she exited.

*****

Craig called Chloe on Monday, around noon, to inform her that the doctors were having difficulties stabilizing his mother's blood pressure. Craig informed Chloe the doctors didn't want to give her any more medicine to bring her blood pressure down until they find out what was causing her heart to beat irregularly. They weren't sure if it's the medication they were using to lower her blood pressure.

"Dad, I am on my way there to the hospital."

"Okay, Chloe. I will further discuss the diagnoses once you arrive."

Chloe called her husband at work to let him know she was heading to the hospital. Robert asked Chloe to drive safe and to call him if she needed anything. Chloe had her classroom assistant take over the class until the substitute teacher arrived.

Forty minutes later, Chloe arrived at the hospital. Tears roll down Chloe's cheeks as she embraced her dad. Craig held Chloe in his arms for a few minutes. He whispered in a calm voice, "She is still here with us. They moved her to intensive care."

Craig and Chloe walked hand in hand toward Mother Baker's room. When they arrived, the doctors were there discussing Mother Baker's condition and making notes in the system. Craig asked the doctors the result of the test in finding the cause of her irregular heartbeats. The head doctor talked as his assistant nodded his head in agreement.

"The results yield no conclusions on the cause of the irregular heartbeat. The heart beating faster with periodic skips could be caused by the high blood pressure. We would like to continue with the medication to lower the blood pressure with hopes in regulating the heart."

Craig agreed with the doctor's decision in lowering his mother's blood pressure.

Craig and Chloe sat in the room with Mother Baker for hours, waiting to see if the medicine would help her condition for the better. Chloe read the Bible to Mother Baker as she laid unconscious. Craig called family members on the phone, updating them about Mother Baker's condition. Mother Baker moved slightly as Chloe read from the book of John, chapter 3. Craig ended his phone conversation as he noticed how his mother was moving. Chloe looked at her dad and nodded as she kept reading. Mother Baker hummed a soft harmony as Chloe read verses 15 through 21 in John chapter 3, "'That whosoever believeth in him should not perish, but have eternal life. For God so loved the world, that he gave his only begotten Son, that whosoever believeth in him should not perish, but have everlasting life. For God sent not his Son into the world to condemn the world; but that the world through him might be saved. He that believeth on him is not condemned: but he that believeth not is condemn already; because he hath not believed in the name of the only begotten Son of God. And this is the condemnation, that light is come into the world, and men loved darkness rather than light, because their deeds were evil. For every one that doeth evil hateth the light, neither cometh to the light, lest his deeds should be reproved. But he that doeth truth cometh to the light, that his deeds may be made manifest, that they are wrought in God.'"

Craig remained silent but moved his hand in a circular motion, expressing to Chloe to continue to read. Mother Baker opened her eyes as Chloe read in John chapter 4, verses 10 through 15, "'Jesus answered and said unto her, If thou knewest the gift of God, and who it is that saith to thee, Give me to drink; thou wouldest have asked of him, and he would have given thee living water. The woman saith unto him, Sir, thou hast nothing to draw with, and the well is deep: from whence then hast thou that living water? Art thou greater than our father Jacob, which gave us the well, and drank thereof himself, and his children, and his cattle? Jesus answered and said unto her, Whosoever drinketh of this water shall thirst again: But whosoever drinketh of the water that I shall give him shall never thirst: but the water that I shall give him shall be in him a well of water springing up into everlasting life. The woman saith unto him, Sir, give me this water, that I thirst not, neither come hither to draw.'"

Craig pushed the button to call for the nurse. The nurse entered the room as Chloe was reading verse 24 of chapter 4. Immediately, upon the presence of the nurse, as Chloe was reading verse 24, "'God is spirit: and they that worship him must worship him in spirit and in truth,'" Mother Baker reopened her eyes as she spoke in her heavenly language.

The nurse stood frozen without saying anything as she identified with the language of tongues. Tears ran down Mother Baker's face as Chloe continued reading verses 25 through 26, "'The woman saith unto him, I know that Messias cometh, which is called Christ: when he is come, he will tell us all things. Jesus saith unto her, I that speak unto thee am he.'"

After reading verse 26, Mother Baker closed her eyes as her spirit was lifted up. The nurse checked Mother Baker's heart with her stethoscope. The nurse immediately called a code blue to the nurse's station. Others nurses ran into the room, including a doctor. They asked Chloe and Craig to move away from the bed as they tried to revive Mother Baker.

After a few minutes, Craig shouted, "Stop! She is gone. Please let her go in peace."

The doctor did one more electric shock when he looked up at Craig to say, "You are right. Your mother is clinically deceased."

The doctor noted the time of death as 7:17 p.m. Craig and Chloe kissed Mother Baker as they said their goodbyes. They embraced each other with tears running down their faces. They were at peace because they knew Mother Baker was at peace.

Craig and Chloe waited for the coroner to come and declare Mother Baker's death. Craig signed the death certificate. Chloe insisted that her dad come home with her. Craig agreed.

The first nurse that entered the room asked Chloe which scriptures of the Bible she was reading from upon her arrival in the room. Chloe wrote the scriptures down and handed it to the nurse. The nurse said she believes God used Mother Baker to minister to her before she departed from this earth. Chloe asked the nurse what made her come to that conclusion. The nurse expressed to Chloe and Craig, "I am an ex-stripper who paid my way through nursing school with the money I made as a stripper. I'm not prove of the things I did as a stripper. I recently joined a church in hopes of forgiveness for the things I did as a stripper. After joining the church, I continued to feel guilt and shame. I began to believe the feeling of guilt and shame was God's way of saying my sins are too great for forgiveness. But three weeks ago, while sitting in church, I had decided to quit coming to church. I had convinced myself that it was useless when God is telling me that my sins are too great to forgive. As I was exiting the church, I heard a voice say to ask God for a sign that he has forgiven me. I immediately turned around to see who had spoken those words in my ear. To my surprise, no one was near me. I heard this same voice speak into my ear when Mother Baker was talking in her heavenly language of tongues. The voice said, 'Whosoever drink of the water of the world, the water of guilt and shame shall thirst again; but whosoever drink of the living water of the son of God shall never thirst.' I immediately felt a sense of peace and knew that God was telling me that my sins were forgiven when I accepted Jesus Christ as my Lord and Savior six months ago. After acknowledging within my spirit that God was talking to me, I heard the same voice speak to my spirit, 'Women, your faith has made you whole.' I now know that I am forgiven."

Chloe hugged the nurse. She then told the nurse about her mom's nonprofit. She gave the nurse a business card with the nonprofit address and phone number. She told the nurse that she was welcome to come share her testimony with other women who are still drinking from the water of guilt and shame.

After Chloe got her dad settled into the guest bedroom, she called her mom. Rose immediately answered the phone. "Chloe, is Mother Baker at rest?"

"Yes, Mom, she is. How did you know?"

"I felt this urgency to pray around 7:00 p.m. I did not cease from praying until around 7:17 p.m. when a sudden wave of peace came over me."

"Mom, Grandmother's time of death was noted at 7:17 p.m."

"Chloe, she is at peace. I know you know."

"Yes, Mom. I know."

"Please know that I am here to assist in any way you and Craig need me. I love you both dearly and want you to know my prayers are with you both."

"Thanks, Mom. I will call you tomorrow. I'm going to rest after I spend some alone time with God."

Rose called Craig immediately after hanging up with Chloe.

"Hello, Rose."

"Craig, my deepest condolences is with you and Chloe. I know it has been a long day for you and Chloe; therefore, I will end this call with the same words I expressed to Chloe. I love you both dearly and want you to know my prayers are with you both. Although, we are not married any longer, we are still family. I am here for you and Chloe."

"Thank you, Rose. I love you as well."

Rose called JJ before letting Janice know about Mother Baker. JJ and Janice both agreed to wait until tomorrow to call Chloe after Rose told them that she was in communion with God and needed a little time alone. Rose also called Barbara to offer her condolences. Barbara and Rose talked briefly about Mother Baker. Barbara expressed how Mother Baker was her favorite aunt.

It was hard for Rose to sleep that night. She laid in bed thinking about the difference between James Sr. and Craig, as well as their family dynamics.

Craig arose early the next day. To his surprise, Chloe was already up. He asked Chloe if she got any sleep. After seeing her up so early, he wasn't surprised to hear that she did not sleep a wink.

Chloe's husband offered to stay home to assist Craig and Chloe. Craig thanked Robert but declined. "Although this is a time of mourning, let's not sit around idle in mourning. My mother was a woman who believed an idle mind is the devil's workshop. Chloe and I would let you know if we need anything. In the meantime, continue living life as you know it. You doing this will help us."

Robert hugged his father-in-law as he agreed to do exactly what was asked of him.

Rose came over to Chloe's home early before heading to work to bring breakfast to her and Craig. She surprised them with bagels with cream cheese, muffins, hash browns, turkey sausages, and orange juice. She offered to cook them some eggs. Craig asked if she could prepare his eggs easy-over. Chloe wanted her eggs scrambled. Chloe put coffee on as Rose prepared the eggs. Robert grabbed a muffin and juice as he ran out the door to work. Rose left for work after having breakfast with Craig and Chloe.

Later that morning, JJ and Janice called Chloe. JJ offered to stop by on his lunch to bring them lunch, and Janice agreed to come by after she got off work. Craig made an afternoon appointment with a local mortuary. And as promised, JJ arrived around 12:30 p.m. with lunch. JJ, Chloe, and Craig reminisced about the good times they had as a family under one roof. They also shared fun memories of Mother Baker. JJ offered to gift the flower arrangements for Mother Baker's homegoing service. Craig and Chloe gladly accepted JJ's offer.

Ninety minutes after JJ's arrival, Craig excused himself to attend his afternoon meeting with the mortuary. Chloe offered to drive her dad, and they all exited together. Because Craig handled his mother's finances, he was able to provide all the information needed to the mortuary. He allowed Chloe to handle the logistics of the service. Chloe ordered a beautiful white with gold trimming casket. She agreed to email a picture of Mother Baker for the program, and she requested a high-grade glossy coated white paper trimmed in gold for the program with black print, an open wing dove on the front and back pages with gold roses on the inside pages. Craig's church agreed to host the service one week from the date at 2:00 p.m.

The mortuary scheduled to pick up Mother's Baker body from the hospital after Craig signed the documents. After the arrangements were made with the mortuary, Chloe took her dad back to her home. Chloe asked her dad to consider moving back in town after Mother Baker's service. She offered him to move into her guest bedroom permanently."

Chloe, your offer is admirable. But how would Robert feel about having his father-in-law living with him and his wife?"

"Dad, Robert and I have discussed the idea of you moving back in town, in our home, on several different occasions. I have been talking to Robert about how much I missed you ever since you moved four hours away after the finalization of your and Mom's divorce. You are no stranger to Robert. He was around you and the family throughout our dating in high school and college. Robert was the one who suggested you move into our guest bedroom."

"It has been a long lonely three years since your mother and I divorced. It would be good to be back around family. Let's discuss it with Robert at dinner tonight before I make a final decision."

"Sounds good, Dad."

*****

Janice arrived at Chloe house around 6:00 p.m. with catered food she picked up from one of Chloe's favorite restaurants. Janice ordered baked chicken, beef tri-tips, baby red potatoes, and asparagus. She bought a cheesecake for dessert with a variety of fruit toppings packaged separately. She greeted Chloe, Craig, and Robert with a hug and expressed her condolences and offered to help in any way needed.

The food was still hot. Janice offered to say the blessing before they ate. Everyone nodded in agreement.

"Heavenly Father, thank you for allowing your light to illuminate the pathway in seeking spiritual truth when one is in darkness. Thank you for healing emotional wounds and for the love and patience of family. Father, I ask, in the name of your Son and our Savior, Jesus Christ, that you bless each person's presence here with the request of their hearts. I pray that you camp your guardian angels around my sister, Chloe, and my stepfather, Craig, to aid them as they celebrate Mother Baker's coming-home-to-you service. And Father, lastly, I ask in Jesus's name that you bless this food that we are about to receive. May everyone present in agreement shout 'amen.'"

Everyone, in unison, shouted "Amen!"

Craig thanked Janice for a beautiful, powerful prayer. To his surprise, Janice hugged him as she stated, "You are welcome. It was my honor." Craig could see the works of God in Janice's presence. He noticed she wasn't the same girl he helped in raising. She had a spiritual glow that illuminated her aura. Her disposition was softer and more welcoming. He felt a sense of peace and comfort being around her.

After they ate dinner, Janice asked Craig if she could talk to him in private on the patio in the backyard. Craig escorted Janice to the patio. He pulled a chair from the patio table for her to sit. He sat on the other side of the table facing Janice.

"Craig, thank you for allowing me to have this private conversation with you. The evening is late for a workday, so I won't be long. I want to personally apologize to you for all the trouble and disrespect I had toward you when you were married to Mom. You did not do anything to warrant the rude, disrespectable behavior I always had toward you. You have always been respectful, kind, and generous toward me, regardless of the ugliness I expressed toward you. I now realize I missed out on a lot of fun with you had I open my heart. I cannot turn back the hands of time and change the past, but I pray you accept my apology so that moving forward, I can enjoy the gentle soul before me. Please forgive me, Craig, and please accept my apology."

"Janice, I accept your forgiveness and apology. I know I'm not your biological dad, but I have always thought of you as my daughter. I loved you in your flaws, and I promise to love you more in this new light I see around you. I know you have to go to work tomorrow. Let me walk you out to your car."

Craig escorted Janice back in the house. After Janice kissed Chloe and Robert goodnight, she allowed Craig to escort her out. Chloe could see, by looking at Janice's and Craig's faces, the talk between them was pleasant. She wasn't sure what happened to bring on the sudden change, but she was elated to see it taking place. Growing up, she always noticed Janice's rudeness and disrespect toward Craig. She never took a side because she would often think about the scenario being in reverse and she was the one whose dad was dead and having to live with a stepfather whose biological child was her sibling. The pain of the thought helped her to understand Janice.

After Craig came back in from walking Janice out, he asked Chloe and Robert if he could talk with them before retiring for the evening. Chloe turned off the TV in the family room to give her dad their undivided attention. Craig asked Chloe if she had spoken to Robert about the question she asked him earlier today. Chloe smiled at her dad before replying yes.

"Chloe and I were discussing you joining our home as you and Janice talked on the patio."

"How do you feel about me joining your home, Robert?"

"Craig, I have been encouraging Chloe for nearly a year to have you come move in our home with us. Of course she wanted you to come, but she also wanted you to have the time you needed alone to heal from the divorce. Craig, I love you like my dad. You are always welcome in our home. You have always treated me like your son as I dated your daughter. With that being said, my casa is always your casa."

They all laughed out loud.

"Well, I guess it's final. You two have a new roommate. On that note, I going to my room. It has been a long day. Suddenly I'm sleepy."

Chloe and Robert watched the late news before retiring to bed.

The next morning, Craig and Chloe rented a small trailer for moving Craig's clothing and personal belongings to Chloe's home. Craig gave his landowner a thirty-day notice and promised to have the remaining of his things out before the end of the notice. After they unloaded Craig's items in the guest room, Chloe took her dad to return the trailer rental.

That evening, after dinner, Chloe went through Mother Baker's pictures for the program and obituary. She found a picture Mother

Baker had taken in her missionary uniform. The uniform was white with gold trim and buttons. Chloe scanned the picture into her computer then emailed a copy of the picture to the mortuary. She made a list of clothing to purchase and take to the mortuary for Mother Baker's homegoing. She thought it would be easier to buy a wig rather than have someone do her hair. Because there were many distant cousins, Chloe ordered only three-family cars so no one would be offended for not being invited to ride in the family car. The first family car would be for Craig, Chloe, Craig's cousin Barbara with her partner. The second car was for Rose, JJ and his family, and Janice. The third car was for Craig's two nephews who he helped to raise and their spouses.

Rose and Janice offered to host the repast at an Italian restaurant that had a buffet bar. The restaurant had several private rooms for event rentals. Rose and Janice rented a room to hold three hundred people. The rental cost included all-you-could-eat buffet and drinks.

On the day of the service, Rose and Janice packed thirty centerpieces for the tables in their cars. The family met at the Italian restaurant thirty minutes before the family service cars were scheduled to arrive. Rose and Janice arrived an hour before the family service cars so that they could unload the centerpieces and give the restaurant final instructions for the event.

As the family service cars arrived, everyone exited their personal cars. The family arrived at the church five minutes before the service was scheduled to start. They were instructed to remain in the car until the procession was ready to begin.

The service was two hours. During the ending procession, the attendees were asked to remain in their seats until the ushers escorted them out by rolls. They were given instructions on where to join the caravan lineup for police escort to the burial. The burial took approximately thirty minutes. After the burial, the caravan of people was instructed to read their program for the address and directions to the repast. Each person at the burial was given a wristband to get in the private repast.

The family service cars took the family back to the restaurant. To the family's surprise, there were people at the restaurant requesting access to the private event before the family arrived. The staff at the restaurant asked the family how they would like them to handle the crowd. Craig asked his two nephews, JJ, and a couple of his cousin sons to monitor the doors, only allowing the two hundred people with a wristband in and the first eighty people in line holding a program. He asked them to apologize to all others because they only accommodated room for three hundred people.

The first eighty people in line holding a program where given wristbands to come in the event. All others were turned away. No one recognized any of the people who were standing in line at the repast. Craig and his family were only familiar with the people who attended the burial. For this reason, he did not feel too bad having to turn people away. The attendees at the repast was allowed to come up to the mic and tell an uplifting experience they had with Mother Baker as everyone ate. The repast lasted for fifteen hours. Fifteen minutes before the end, the family came up to thank everyone for coming and celebrating the life of Mother Baker with them. They were asked to respect the restaurant staff's guidance as they escorted everyone out the side exit.

A week after Mother Baker's homegoing service, Craig and JJ rented a truck to move the rest of Craig's belonging to storage near Chloe's home. On the ride to pick up the belongings, JJ asked Craig about his cousin Ralph.

"How do you know my cousin Ralph? He is a distant cousin that I don't communicate with or have ever introduce to you all. Ralph has always been a streetwise gangster. It is for this reason I never associated with him. He is the type that would rob his own mama to get what he wants. He is definitely not a good character of people to be around. Why are you asking about him?"

"Well, at the repast, Ralph's daughter, April, introduced herself to me. She claims to work with my dad's younger brother, John. This is my dad's brother who stole their mother's life insurance policy and tried to fraudulently have the policy put in his name. April gave me my uncle John's telephone number with a note from John stating he would like to meet me. I never had a relationship with my dad's siblings. I only know of them from what my dad told me after he had a few drinks. They did not come to my dad's funeral. I do not know if I have cousins on my dad's side of the family. As you know, Mom is an only child, and both her parents are deceased. She doesn't talk about having any extended family. Our family circle is very small, with the exception to your family, which is very large. I often wonder what it is like having a large extended family. Growing up with your two nephews have been a blessing. It gave me some type of interactions with cousins."

"JJ, I understand your desire to know more about your family from a personal perspective. Our experience, whether good or bad, is what makes us who we are as people. As a child, I was curious about fire. I often wondered what makes it hot. I did not know it was hot. I was told it was hot. I decided to experiment by sticking my finger in the fire coming from the stove burner. Before I could immerge my finger into the fire, I felt heat and instant pain as I moved my finger near the fire. The heat and pain felt deterred my decision to fully experience fire. My mother, may she rest in peace, often told me that people have a tendency of thinking that the grass is always greener on the other side. In other words, people cannot see their blessing because they believe their blessing is in what they don't have in their possession.

"Your father spoke his truth to you about his sibling. Him sharing the information after a few drinks doesn't make his experience with his siblings less truthful. I do believe people's characteristics can be distributed differently depending on the relationship with the person. If you asked three strangers to describe the character of a common friend, there may be similar traits noted; however, more than likely, there will be a single trait that is only experienced by the individual making the perception. If you feel the need to have a relationship with your dad's siblings, proceed with caution. Your experience with them may be totally different from your dad's relationship with his siblings. However, don't discount what your dad shared about his siblings. Think of it this way: Why do you tell your son, Trey, to wear protected gear when riding his bike?"

"Thanks, Craig. I'm not sure yet if I will call John. There is this yearning to know more about my dad's side of the family. But I will not discount what you and my dad have said."

After JJ and Craig returned the rental truck, JJ called his mom on the way back home.

"Hi, Mom. Do you have a minute to talk?"

"Hi, JJ. Yes, I have time to talk. Is everything okay?"

"Everything is okay. I need to talk to you about a note I received at the repast from Craig's second cousin, April."

"Okay, when do you want to talk?"

"Can I take you to Sunday brunch tomorrow?"

"Sure."

"Brunch is served from 8:00 a.m. to 2:00 p.m. I will pick you up at 10:00 a.m."

"Sound good, JJ. I will see you tomorrow."

*****

JJ was nervous on the drive to pick up his mom. He wasn't sure how to approach her about wanting to contact his uncle John. He never talked to his mom about family outside of the inner circle.

JJ arrived at 9:50 a.m. to pick up his mom.

"Good morning, JJ. Will Grace and Trey be joining us for brunch?"

"No, ma'am. It's just you and me this morning."

"Not ma'am. Mum!"

"I thought it was time to have some one-on-one time with my mother. We always interact in the surrounding of others. This morning, it's just you and me, Mom."

"Okay, sounds good, JJ. I hope you do not wait until I am full and sleepy before you talk to me about the real purpose of this one-on-one time together."

"I should have known better than to be discrete with you. I would like to wait until we get our food and we are settled before I talk to you about what is on my mind."

"Okay, JJ. Sounds like a plan."

It showed that JJ had learned a lot from his stepdad, Craig. He is the perfect gentleman. He opened the doors for his mom. He pulled out her chair before she sat. Once they were settled with their food and drink, JJ began their conversation with small talk.

"So how do you like the food here, Mom?"

"So far, everything I have tasted is good. How did you find this restaurant? I never knew this hotel had an elegant restaurant that served Sunday brunch."

"A coworker recommended this place."

"Okay, son. Enough of the small talk. You asked me to brunch to discuss a note you received at the repast from Craig's cousin's daughter, April."

"Yes, Mom. April approached me at the repast. She told me that she works with my uncle John, and that he asked her to give me a sealed envelope that contained a typewritten note"

"What is the note about?"

"John introduced himself in the note as my dad's brother. He is requesting to meet and establish a relationship with me."

"How do you feel about John's request?"

"I am complexed."

"Complexed or curious?"

"I am curious as well, Mom. I want to know more about my dad's family. I have always admired Craig's large family unit and often wondered what it was like to have a family beyond you, Janice, Chloe, my wife, and son."

"I have never talked to you about James Sr.'s family. How much do you know about them? I'm sure James has talked with you about them."

"Dad has only told me about why he didn't talk to them. He told me about them stealing his mom's insurance policy."

"Yet knowing this information, your curiosity is steering you in the direction of forming a relationship with them."

"This is why I said I am complexed."

"I think you feeling complexed has nothing to do with what you know about James's family. I think it has everything to do with how I feel about you having a relationship with James's family."

"You know me well, Mom. I need your blessings."

"JJ, you do not need my blessings. My blessings might help you to feel at ease with your concern about your decision. At the end of the day, you are a grown man who does not need his mom telling him if it's okay to be in relationship with his dad's family. However, since you have opened the door for my opinion, I would like to point out a few things for you to consider as you explore your dad's side of the family. With that being said, let me tell you what I am curious about. How did your uncle John know about our relationship with Craig? James wasn't communicating with his family throughout our marriage. I do not believe he communicated with them after he and I divorced. So how does John know about your connection to Craig's cousin's daughter, April? How does John know that you were going to be at the repast? Given what Craig has told me about his cousin Ralph and my interaction with him at the hospital, I am curious to know his relationship with John, as well as his daughter's, April, relationship with John. I know you said they are coworkers; however, I feel there's more to their relationship than being just coworkers. My advice to you, should you pursue this relationship, move cautiously."

"I will consider all your concerns, Mom, and move cautiously."

"I see your decision has been made. I am here as your mother to love you unconditionally without judgment or bias. So please do not feel like you cannot talk to me about your relationship experience with your dad's family. I love you, son."

"I love you too, Mom."

"Do you plan on telling Janice?"

"Because she is currently in counseling dealing with issues pertaining to Dad, I do not want to add more to her plate. I will tell her as she grows stronger from her counseling."

"Okay, JJ. I will respect your wishes. I will leave it to you to talk with your sister about your relationship with James's family. Let's leave this restaurant before they have to wheel me out of here from overeating. The food is very good. Thank you for bringing me here."

"You are welcome, Mom. We should come here on our next scheduled Sunday family dinner."

"Sounds like a winner. I will let you suggest this place to the family."

JJ took Rose back home immediately after leaving the restaurant. He kissed his mom on the cheek after helping her out the car.

*****

As soon as JJ opens his front door, his wife was anxiously waiting to hear how things went with her mother-in-law, Rose.

"Hi, honey. From your expression, it appears all is well between you and your mom."

"Yes, Grace. Things went better than I thought. Of course Mom has her concerns about my dad's side of the family wanting to have a relationship with me; nonetheless, she supports my decision."

"When do you plan on contacting your uncle John?"

"I think now would be a good time."

JJ went to get the note to attain John's phone number. When John saw the name James Jackson on his caller ID, he immediately picked up the call. "Well, hello, nephew. This is your uncle John. When I saw the name on the caller ID, I knew it had to be you."

"Hello, Uncle John."

"It feels good hearing you call me uncle. I have been wanting to meet you for a long time."

"Uncle John, why did you wait so long to reach out to me?"

"Well, James—"

JJ interrupted his uncle, "Everyone calls me JJ."

"Well, JJ, our family unity is not the best. As you probably know, your dad separated himself from his family years ago after our mother died. This was before he met your mother. Mutual friends of ours would keep me up-to-date about James. If it wasn't for the mutual friends, we wouldn't know if your dad was dead or alive."

"Who are you referring to when you say 'we'?"

"I'm referring to your dad's sister, JoAnn, and your dad's other brother, Jack. Our mother, who is your grandmother, gave birth to four kids. Although James was not the oldest, he took on the role as the oldest."

"What do you mean he took on the role?"

"James has always been a go-getter. He always worked odd jobs as a kid when the rest of us were enjoying being kids. He gets this from our dad, who worked himself to death at an early age. After Dad died, James took on the financial responsibilities. He helped Mom to pay the bills and feed us all. Your uncle Jack is the eldest. Since a young boy, Jack was always chasing his dream to become a musician. He would get a lot of local nightclub jobs. Occasionally, he would tour with various artists. After years of off and on working, his wife became frustrated with having to support their family. Jack's wife divorced him then moved to Mississippi with their two kids. The last I heard, Jack had started heavily drinking alcohol and is living on Skid Row.

"Your aunt JoAnn is still married to her high school sweetheart. They have four kids and are living in the government-run housing projects off Monroe Street. We occasionally keep in touch. I don't like going over there because those boys of hers are always in trouble. I'm not trying to go back to jail…that kind of slipped out…

"Anyway, I want you to know I wasn't in jail for any hard crime. I had to serve thirty days in the county jail for petty theft. I was in between jobs and had to feed me and my girl."

"You have a daughter, Uncle Jack?"

"No, I was talking about my girlfriend. I don't have any kids. My wife and I divorced years ago after she had three miscarriages. She blamed me for us not being able to carry our babies' full term. She claimed it was because of the drugs. See, I used to be on drug. I have been clean and sober for ten years. I met my current girlfriend at the sober living group counseling clinic. We both were former addicts. We keep each other balance."

"What is your girlfriend's name, Uncle Jack?"

"My girlfriend's name is April. She is the one who gave you the note from me. We both work as cooks at the sober living facility on Jefferson Boulevard."

"How did April know that I was related to you? Or that I would be at the repast?"

"April's dad, Ralph, and Craig are cousins. Although Ralph and Craig do not socialize with each other, they would occasionally meet at family events that was hosted by Craig's mother, Cassie Baker. Everyone loved and knew of Mother Baker. She spent her life helping the homeless and sober living people. She would have the church buses pick up people to bring them to Bible study on Thursday evenings. After Bible study, she served hot food and give out warm clothing. Mother Baker would come to the sober living facility where April and I worked to preach every Tuesday afternoon before she became ill. Mother Baker always encouraged April and me in our sober living. She helped April and me get the jobs as cooks. Mother Baker asked Craig to help host her last family event. The event was held in a large conference room at the convention center. There were approximately five hundred families and friends at the event. Mother Baker announced that due to help issues, she was retiring. She encouraged everyone to continue to fight the good fight of faith. When she introduced her son, Craig, and gave a little bio on him, she mentioned that he was married for twenty years to Rose Baker and had two stepkids, James Jackson Jr. and Janice Jackson, and one biological daughter, Chloe Baker. She introduced Chloe to everyone and talked about her carrying on the legacy of caring for people as a grade school teacher. I asked April if she ever meet Craig's ex-wife, Rose, and his stepkids. April said no. Then I asked April why the stepkids did not attend the event. April said they live a high-and-mighty life with their mom in the suburbs. I told April that I heard my brother James Jackson had married a girl named Rose, and they had a son together.

"April asked many of her family at the event if they knew of Rose and her kids. April's dad's cousin Barbara said that she knew Rose and her kids well. April asked Barbara if Rose was once married to someone named James Jackson. Barbara said yes then asked April why she wanted to know. April told Barbara she was wondering if he was related to someone she was dating whose last name is Jackson. Barbara looked at April strangely with a half smile then replied, 'Having the same last name doesn't make one related.' April told me that's how people who live in the suburbs act."

"Uncle John, April's observation about people who live in the suburbs is a misconception. My sister and I did not attend the event because we did not know about the event. After Craig and my mom divorced, only Chloe was invited to attend the Baker's family events. I felt left out but never questioned my stepfather, Craig, because I knew it was not his intentions to hurt me or my sister.

"Uncle John, what were your expectations when you wrote the note?"

"JJ, I was hoping to have a relationship with my nephew. I do not have any kids, and I thought it would be encouraging for me and April to be around positive people who are doing good things in life. April and I don't have much, so we cannot offer you what you are accustomed to having."

"What do you mean 'accustomed to having'?"

"Well, April and I would love to invite you over for dinner or take you out to dinner, but we are not in financial position to do so."

"Well, how about my wife and I invite you and April over for dinner?"

"That sounds real good, JJ. April and I would love to come."

"Okay. I will call you next week to schedule a date and time."

"Okay, JJ. Have a good evening."

"You as well, Uncle John. Bye."

After ending the phone call, John told April, "We are in. We just need to stick to the plan."

JJ talked to his wife about the conversation. Although Grace did not like all that she heard, she was committed to supporting her husband. She was concerned about their son, Trey, meeting his great uncle John but agreed to dinner at their home on Saturday.

JJ called his uncle John on Wednesday to invite him and April to dinner on Saturday. John accepted the invite. When JJ gave John his address, John asked if he could be picked up because his car wasn't in the condition to drive long distance. JJ agreed to send a car to pick up him and April. Grace became more apprehensive as JJ updated her about his uncle. Her spirit is very vexed about having him and his girlfriend into their home. She was hoping that this one visit would be enough to satisfy JJ's need to meet his dad's family. She didn't feel that John's intentions were good. She didn't know how to express her concerns to her husband in a supportive manner.

She began to prepare their home for the visit by removing all valuables that could be easily slipped into a bag or purse. She asked JJ to only have them use the guest bathroom and not suggest they use the upstairs bathroom if the guest bathroom was occupied. She asked JJ to not give them a tour of the house or suggest they stay the night. She suggested that they do not serve alcoholic drinks, and that the car is scheduled to take them back home shortly after dinner is over. And if they were to have any other dinner gathering with them, it should be done at a restaurant. JJ realized at that moment that Grace was really concerned about having his uncle in their home. He did not know this dinner had such an ill effect on Grace. Had he known this was how she felt, he would have arranged to meet with them at a restaurant but thought it would look suspicious if he changed the plans one day before they are scheduled to come for dinner. JJ prayed for the best.

The car arrived at 5:00 p.m. with John and April. John was grinning from ear to ear as he met JJ for the first time. He stood back and looked at JJ.

"Boy, you look just like your daddy."

JJ smiled. JJ could see a slight resemblance John had to his dad. Suddenly, JJ thought, *How do I really know this is my uncle? I only talked to him twice over the phone, and I've never seen a picture of him.* The words that Craig and his mom spoke to him suddenly hit him in his gut: *proceed with caution.* However, JJ did recognize April as the person who gave him the note and began to relax.

JJ introduced John and April to Grace and Trey. April recalled seeing Grace at the repast but did not know she was JJ's wife. JJ invited them to sit in the family room as Grace offered them a drink. Before Grace could finish her sentence as to what she had to drink, John and April were asking if they had rum and coke. Grace apologized for misleading them into thinking they had alcoholic drinks. She rephrased her question, "Would you like a soda? Some punch or water? We also have sparkling cider." Both John and April turned up their noses and agreed to wait until dinner was served to have something to drink. John asked for a tour of the house. Grace looked at JJ before stating "There isn't much to see. JJ, do you want to show them the ground floor and the patio area?" JJ escorted them around in the direction of the backyard.

"Boy, this is nice!" shouted John.

"I told you it would be nice in the suburbs," declared April.

Grace announced that dinner was ready. She invited them into the dining room as she placed the serving dishes on the table.

"I hope you two like pot roast and baked chicken."

"We get to have two meats!" shouted April.

"Well, I wanted you to have a choice of one or both."

Grace also prepared scalloped potatoes, steamed yellow and green squash, sautéed string beans with mushrooms and baby pearl onions, and salad with a variety of salad dressing. Trey was given a baked chicken leg with a small portion of scalloped potatoes and some steamed squash. April asked if that was all Trey was going to eat.

"Trey is only three and a half. He doesn't eat much at one sitting. He has snacks throughout the day," replied Grace.

John and April looked at each other. Grace did not understand why the weird look.

JJ asked John where he and April lived.

"Right now, we are living in a studio apartment. We are on the waiting list for a nice newly built two-bedroom government-subsidized housing apartment near the downtown area."

Grace questioned how they met the government requirements for a two-bedroom apartment. She only knew the government to qualify people as an individual or as a family.

"We secretly got married six months ago to qualify as a family for the apartment."

"Do you have kids?" asked Grace.

"No, we are approved to foster a child."

Grace's spirit did not sit right with their answers. She did not understand why their marriage was a secret. April told JJ that the note she gave him was from a coworker. John introduced April as his girlfriend. Grace did not trust these two.

Grace was starting to feel uncomfortable with the lies and decided to make an excuse for them to leave. Grace looked at JJ and asked, "What time will the car be here to pick up John and April? I want to package to-go containers for them. This is too much food for us to eat ourselves."

JJ texted for the car. The driver said he was ten minutes away. Grace asked April if she would like to help her package to-go containers for them. April was happy to help. April practically packaged all the pot roast and most of the chicken. Grace gave her the whole cheesecake she purchased for dessert to package. Grace did not care if they took all the food; she wanted them out of her home.

Ten minutes later, JJ was escorting them to the car, helping them carry their package food containers. After John and April left, JJ and Grace cleaned the kitchen before putting Trey to bed. They poured themselves a glass of wine as they discussed the evening. They both agreed that something wasn't right with their story. They couldn't understand what it had to do with them but felt those two somehow wanted to include them in whatever scheme they had going. Grace made JJ promise to never invite them to their home again. JJ agreed with Grace.

JJ had a complex look on his face as he filled his canteen with coffee before heading to work. Grace calling his name startled him.

"You were deep in thought. Is everything okay?"

"Yes. I was just thinking about this coming Sunday."

"What about it?"

"We come together as a family to share a meal."

"What is so complex about us coming together?"

"Nothing. I was recalling the conversation I had with Mom. She asked me to set up the next family gathering since I recommended brunch at the same restaurant I took her. Also, I was wondering if we should invite Craig now that he is living with Chloe. Also, I am concerned about Craig or Mom asking me in front of Janice about meeting with Uncle John. You know I am not ready to let Janice know about Uncle John contacting me until I know she is doing well with her counseling."

"I think you should talk to Mom about inviting Craig. I'm sure she will be okay with you inviting him. Also, I think you should ask Mom and Craig to not mention your uncle John until you have a chance to talk with Janice."

"Sounds good. I will call everyone today."

Around midday, JJ remembered he needed to call the family. He called his mom first to get her input on him inviting Craig. Rose was elated about JJ inviting Craig. Everyone agreed to meeting at the restaurant for brunch. JJ reserved a table for eight people.

That evening, after dinner, JJ and Grace decided to type fun questions on strips of paper as conversational entertainment during brunch. Each strip of paper was folded separately and placed in a small lid container. As they settled for the evening, someone knocked on their front door before ringing the doorbell. The aggressive knocking startled them because they weren't expecting anyone and knew from the sound of the knock that it was with an urgency. JJ looked out the narrow glass window next to the front door. He saw a man and women dressed in business attire with two police officers. He assumed they had the wrong address as he opened the door.

"Hello. How may I help?"

"Are you James Jackson?" asked the man.

"Yes. Who are you?"

"I am Mr. Brown and this is Ms. Cooper. We are from child protective service. We are here to do a wellness check on James Jackson III. According to our notes, he is called Trey."

"I am confused. Why would someone feel that our son needs a wellness check?"

"We are not at liberty to discuss the details of the wellness check. Can you please allow us to do our job?"

Grace began to cry and shouted, "You are not coming in our home to do a wellness check. This is an insult to the love and care we give to our son. How dare someone question the care of our son!"

The police interjected, "Ma'am, you need to allow these people do their job so we all can enjoy the rest of our evening."

JJ and Grace allowed everyone at the door to enter their home. Ms. Cooper escorted Grace upstairs to get Trey. Ms. Cooper looked around Trey's room while taking notes. Ms. Cooper asked to see Trey's bare chest, back, arms, and legs. Then she asked how much Trey weighs and his age and height. Grace looked at Ms. Cooper strangely.

"You look familiar."

"I don't live on this side of town. I'm here do my job," replied Ms. Cooper.

Grace noticed Ms. Cooper shifted in her disposition and became a little nervous. Ms. Cooper hurried back down the stairs. Mr. Brown greeted her, asking where the child Trey was. Ms. Cooper stated, "I did the wellness check. We can leave." Mr. Brown looked complex before saying okay. Mr. Brown told JJ and Grace to have a good evening as they all exited the home.

"I wonder what that was all about," stated JJ.

"I do not know. But I will get to the bottom of this."

Grace told JJ about what happened upstairs and how Ms. Cooper became extremely nervous after mentioning she looked familiar. JJ did not know what to think but did not want to speculate.

"Grace, let's stay calm. We know as parents that we are not doing anything to harm our child. Truth will always win. Let's get some sleep and try to put this behind us."

Grace couldn't promise that she would put this behind them, so she remained silent as she headed back upstairs to bed.

*****

The family met at 10:30 a.m. at the restaurant. After everyone was sitting comfortably with their plate of food, Grace explained the rules of the game. The container would be passed around to one person at a time. Each person would take one strip of paper containing a question. The question could be answered truthfully or the answer could be fabricated. Everyone would have to vote if the answer is true or false. The person answering the question would receive one point for each person they were able to deceive with their answer. The person with the most points would receive a $25 gift card from a place of their choice from each person who participated in the game. The game was over when the waiter picked up the check. Names would be put in a cup to draw in the event of a tie.

Grace felt this game would be a good distraction from Thursday evening's wellness check. She did not want to put a damper on the family gathering, although she was eager to tell them all what happened.

Craig was so happy to be back together with the family. He couldn't remember the last time he had so much fun. He knew it was before the divorce but had allowed loneliness and sadness rob him of his fun memories. They all laughed together and enjoyed each other's company.

Everyone could see the change in Janice. She allowed herself to fully enjoy each person's presence, especially Craig. Rose was elated to see how much Janice had transition for the better since starting counseling with Dr. Ruth.

Janice was the winner of the game. Because of her transformation, it was hard for the family to know if her answers were true or false. She asked the family to surprise her with a gift card from one of their favorite places to shop. Janice's plan was to regift their card with a personal gift she would buy each one for Christmas from their favorite place to shop. She would know where each person liked to shop based on the gift card she would receive from them.

Before exiting the restaurant, Rose offered to host Thanksgiving at her home. She volunteered to prepare turkey with stuffing and a ham. She asked everyone else to bring side dishes. They all agreed to send a group text one week before Thanksgiving of what each person was bringing and to be at Rose's home around 1:00 p.m. on Thanksgiving Day. With Thanksgiving being two and a half weeks away, each person had a little over one week to send their group text.

As promised, the family was group texting side dishes. Grace was bringing her famous scalloped potatoes and green bean casserole. Chloe was bringing collard greens with smoked turkey necks and candied yams. Janice was preparing mac 'n' cheese and potato salad. Craig agreed to order dessert from the farmer's bakery. JJ would bring alcoholic drinks, and Robert would bring nonalcoholic drinks.

On the morning of Thanksgiving, JJ received a call from his uncle John.

"Hello, Uncle John. How are you?"

"Hey, man. I'm good. What are you and your family up to this morning?"

"Well, the morning is early. We are barely out of bed."

"I mean, what are your plans for the day? I was hoping April and I can come back over today for Thanksgiving dinner."

"Uncle John, Grace and I will not be having dinner at our home today. We have been invited elsewhere. Grace and I promise to take you and April out to dinner at a later time. Maybe we can plan something for this weekend after Thanksgiving."

"So you are saying that we cannot join you where you are going for Thanksgiving?"

"Uncle John, I think it would be best if we all got together at a later time."

"Okay, man. I see where this conversation is going. I wouldn't hold my breath waiting on you to call me for dinner."

"Uncle John, I am a man of my word. I have a private invite today and do not think it would be a good idea to bring others to a private event."

"Okay, JJ. April is in my ear telling me your way is how people in the suburbs handle parties. In the hood, we are open to bringing whoever we want to a party. We don't call them private. Okay, man. I will talk to you later."

JJ told Grace about his phone conversation with his uncle John. Grace asked JJ, "When are you going to believe what everyone has been telling you about your father's family? You cannot bring back the relationship you had with your father through his siblings. Although they grew up in the same household, their morals and values are totally different."

JJ sadly agreed with Grace.

*****

JJ was happy to take his mind off his father's family at Thanksgiving dinner at his mom's home. The atmosphere was pleasant and joyful. The family was enjoying each other's company, when around 8:00 p.m., JJ's cell phone rang nonstop. JJ recognized it was his security monitoring service calling.

"Hello," JJ eagerly answer the call.

"Hello, Mr. Jackson. Sorry to bother you on Thanksgiving, but your home alarm has been buzzing for approximately five minutes. We called your home phone and did not receive an answer. We have dispatched the police to your home. They are there now checking the grounds. Can you verify your code so we can disarm your alarm?"

JJ gave the caller his code and informed the caller that he was on his way home.

"Mr. Jackson, would you like for us to stay on the phone with you until you arrive home?"

"No, I will be all right."

"Okay, Mr. Jackson. We will email you a copy of the police report with their findings."

Everyone followed behind JJ to his house. Upon their arrival, the police had one man handcuffed sitting on the curb as flashlights were moving around the perimeters of his house. JJ walked up to the two policeman standing near the man sitting on the curb. The policeman asked JJ if he was the owner. JJ answered yes. He was instructed to show ID. JJ handed the policeman his driver's license. The policeman asked JJ who the other people with him were. JJ answered, "They are my family."

The policeman asked JJ if he know the man sitting on the curb.

"I've never seen this man in my life."

The police asked JJ's family if they knew the man. The man looked familiar to Craig, but he wasn't sure and did not want to speculate. The policeman told JJ that neighbors saw three men. The other two men got away, but they had hopes of finding out who they were. They informed JJ that the attempted break-in was unsuccessful, and that his neighbors were a big help in scaring off the intruders by releasing their dogs to chase after the men.

"This is how we caught this one. He went up a tree and couldn't get down because the dogs had him surrounded. The other two probably drove off. We found tire skid marks a quarter block down your street. Our report will be available in twenty-four hours. Your windows and doors are secured. We did not find any signs of break-in. If you like, a police officer could accompany you inside."

JJ declined.

According to his online security monitoring system, no windows or doors were successfully opened. The intruders tried to open a back window when the alarm went off.

After the police left, the family went into JJ's home. Craig asked JJ if he wanted him to stay the night with them. JJ assured everyone that they would be okay. Grace wanted to tell everyone about JJ's uncle John. She wanted them to know he knew of them not being home, and that she was suspicious of him.

Craig told JJ, "We need to talk later. Let's get together on Saturday for coffee."

JJ agreed.

*****

JJ was surprised to receive an early morning call from John, canceling their dinner plan with him and Grace. John claimed he and April had other plans. JJ was relieved because he knew Grace did not want to meet for dinner with John and April.

JJ's thoughts flashed back to Craig asking to have coffee with him. He called Craig to see what time was good for him. Craig offered to buy JJ lunch at the local café. They agreed to meet at noon.

When JJ arrived at the café, Craig was sitting at the table, waiting.

"Hi, Craig. How long have you been waiting?"

"I arrived two minutes ago. You are right on time."

They both ordered the soup and sandwich combo.

"I know you are wondering why I asked to talk with you, so let me skip the small talk and get to the point. The person who were apprehended by the police at your home on Thanksgiving looked familiar. He looks like someone who associates with my cousin Ralph's son, RJ. RJ is just as untrustworthy as his father. RJ is known for hanging around thugs. Because it has been over ten years since I last saw RJ or his thug friends, I wasn't 100 percent sure when the police asked if anyone knew the guy. Also, I questioned in my mind, how would RJ and his thug friends know your address, when I suddenly remembered April gave you a note from your uncle John; and it is quite possible you gave your uncle John your home address."

"You are right, Craig. I was looking for the right time to talk with the family about my meeting with Uncle John. Many unexplainable occurrences have been happening since meeting with Uncle John and April."

"April! Why are you meeting with April?"

"Well, we came to find out April and John are a couple, as well as cooks working for the same sober living facility."

"So that's the connection."

"Yes, April is the bridge that connects my uncle John to your family."

JJ continued to tell Craig about dinner at his house with John and April and the unexplainable occurrences. Craig believed John and April were behind all the occurrences.

"JJ, I cannot tell you what to do; however, I am suggesting that you limit your face-to-face contact with John and April, and that you use wisdom when having a phone conversation. Criminal-minded people listen to every word you say in hopes to use something you said against you for their benefit. The devil is real, and his spirit dwells among those who are easily influenced by his presence. We all have free will to choose God or the devil. Unfortunately, many choose the devil. The Bible tells us in Matthew 10:16, 'To be therefore wise as serpents, and harmless as doves.' God does not ask something of you that he hasn't equipped you with, so use the wisdom of his Holy Spirit to guide you. Do not allow newly found family guilt you into proving your worthiness to them because a family that is rooted in godly principles would not make you feel bad about the blessings of God. Also, I think you should talk to your family about what has transpired since meeting with John and April. You need prayer warriors interceding on your behalf."

"Thanks, Craig. I agree with you. I will call a family meeting so I can tell everyone at once. My prayer is that this doesn't rescind the progress Janice has made in her counseling sessions."

"Janice will be all right. Her eyes are open. The spirit of God is with her. God did not open her eyes to make her weak."

"Thank you for allowing God to use you in helping to open my eyes."

JJ was feeling much better about having a discussion with the family regarding John and April. JJ shared his lunch meeting with his wife, Grace. Grace was elated that someone in the family other than her knew what was going on. Once the other family members have been informed, she would have someone other than JJ hearing her concerns.

*****

Two weeks prior to Christmas, the family met at JJ's house for Sunday dinner. JJ used the opportunity to tell the family about John and April. Rose remained silent. JJ asked his mom what her thoughts were.

"I'm happy you met with Craig to share with him all the things that have occurred since meeting with John and April. I'm happy that Craig is a God-fearing man, who guided you with wisdom. I'm happy Craig is back in our lives because his presence is needed."

Rose began to cry. Craig gave Rose a hug as he whispered in her ear, "I will always be here for you and the kids. I love you, Rose."

Rose whispered back in Craig's ear, "I love you, Craig."

Janice got up from her seat to give Craig and her mom a hug. As she returned to her seat, she expressed her thoughts.

"Sometimes it's difficult for one to see the love in front of them when one is thinking about the love not received elsewhere. I am guilty of this. But I thank God my eyes and heart are now open. JJ, Dad's brother John has reiterated what Dad warned you about regarding his family. Do not beat up on yourself for not using pre-conceived information to judge someone's character. With time, some people change for the better, while others become craftier in wickedness. I understand we cannot blame John and April without evidence for the occurrences that had happened since meeting them; however, I am receiving the same gut feeling as Grace. Those two are linked to what has happened."

Chloe began to shift in her seat. JJ asked her for her thoughts.

"Although I have never socialized with cousin Ralph or his kids outside of Mother Baker's family events, my spirit always felt vexed whenever I encountered them at the events. What you all don't know is that Ralph approached Mom in a negative way at the hospital during

Mother Baker's surgery. Dad had to ask him to leave. Ralph was angry Mom was present among the family at the hospital. He called her 'high-and-mighty thinking' and told her she needed to leave."

Chloe's statement made JJ recall a phrase April often used. JJ decided to share it with the family.

"April would often state in conservation, 'That's how they are in the suburbs' when commenting on something I said or on actions I take or on an assumption in her thoughts."

Grace felt comfortable in sharing that Ms. Cooper from the child protective service looked very familiar. She also shared how Ms. Cooper changed in her disposition when stating she looked familiar by stating, "I do not live on this side of town," as well as her sudden eagerness to leave.

"Speaking of Ms. Cooper," stated JJ, "she has left three letters taped to our door since the wellness check. The letters are stating that she is following up on James Jackson III and needs us to contact the office. Each time, Grace or I called her direct number noted on the letter, we get her voicemail. We have left several voice messages. Grace called child protective service's main number only to be transferred by the operator to Ms. Cooper's voicemail. Looking at the time on our video camera, Ms. Cooper came to our home between 9:00 a.m. and 10:00 a.m. to tape the letter to the door. She never rang the doorbell or knock on the door. Which leaves me with the assumption that she knew we were not at home."

Craig stood up and began to speak, "The day has been long. Before we close out this family gathering, let's join hands in prayer. For the Bible declares in Matthew 18:20, 'For where two or three are gathered together in my name, there am I in the midst of them.' Based on what we all have shared here this evening, let's join each other in spirit at the throne of grace, praying that this plot of the adversary against JJ, Grace, and Trey will not prosper. I will start the prayer. The person to my right will pray next until each person in the circle has prayed."

After praying, with tears in their eyes, the family hugged JJ, Grace, and Trey as they all prepared to leave. They all agreed to meet at Chloe's house for Christmas. Chloe would prepare the meat as everyone else would bring the sides. She informed them that she would prepare a ham, a pot roast, and grilled lamb chops. She asked that they follow the same protocol as Thanksgiving by texting the sides each person was bringing one week before Christmas.

JJ decided to take off work on Monday to purchase a tree for Grace to decorate. He would need to drive two hours away to a farm that grew trees for the holiday. He would have a hand in cutting down the tree of his choice. Because Trey's child care center would be closing on Friday for the remaining of the year due to the holiday season, Grace had scheduled vacation time to be home with Trey. She and Trey would decorate the tree together while drinking hot chocolate and eating cookies. She was excited about sharing this time with Trey on his fourth birthday.

As JJ headed out the door around 9:00 a.m., he saw Ms. Cooper walking back to her car after taping another letter on his door. He called her name. She turned around and looked surprised to see him. She jumped in her car and drove away, burning rubber. JJ could not understand why she was leaving these letters and would not return their calls. He told himself the letters could not be to significant if she was not returning their calls or showing up again with the police.

Around 3:00 p.m., JJ had returned home with the tree and some additional decorations to add to what they had in storage. Also, he had picked up Trey's Christmas presents. JJ wasn't sure if he wanted to tell Grace about the letter. He did not want to upset her. He wanted his family to enjoy the holiday season free of worry.

On Friday, as Grace was enjoying the day with Trey, her phone began to ding. It was the family texting their side dishes for Christmas dinner. Because everyone loved Janice's mac 'n' cheese, she decided to prepare it for Christmas. Rose was preparing a peach cobbler, sweet potato pies, mashed potatoes, and fresh sautéed green beans with bacon bits and pearl onions. Grace decided to prepare the collard green with smoked meat and a spring mix green salad with a variety of dressings. The family had emailed to Grace personal videos wishing Trey a happy birthday. JJ had picked up the family's birthday gift to Trey earlier in the week. After dinner, Grace would allow Trey to open each person's gift, following their personal video.

Because Christmas was on a Sunday, the family had agreed to attend the sunrise 6:00-a.m. church service. They like attending the sunrise service because it was only an hour long. The praise team would come out at 6:05 a.m. to usher everyone in song into the presence of God. Following the praise team, the preacher would come out and preach the Word of God for forty minutes. The preacher would end his sermon with altar call and an invitation to new potential members. No later than 7:15 a.m., the congregation were heading out the door as workers were arriving in preparation for the 10:30 a.m. service, which was two and a half hours in length.

The family gathered at Chloe's house around 2:00 p.m. They took a moment to reflect on the meaning of Christmas. Each person quoted one of their favorite scripture from the Bible with a brief explanation why that particular scripture held a special meaning to them. After dinner, they exchanged gifts and played games. By 10:00 p.m., they were exhausted from the long day and grateful they all had Monday off because most businesses closed on Monday due to Christmas falling on a Sunday. Because the family would attend the New Year's Eve watching night service at the church, they would not be attending New Year's Day Sunday morning service at church.

Rose agreed to host New Year's Day brunch at her home. She agreed to keep it simple with fresh fruit, Greek yogurt, granola, Danishes, eggs, grits, waffles, sliced ham, turkey sausage, and bacon. She asked Grace to bring orange juice and Chloe to bring champagne. Janice would pick up another bag of the holiday blend of coffee from their favorite coffee shop.

The family arrived around 10:00 a.m. on New Year's Day. After praying together, the family enjoyed brunch while listening to one of the bishop's sermons. After eating, the topic of discussion was New Year's Resolutions. Some family members shared their current New Year's Resolutions and the reason for the resolution. Other shared some of their old resolutions. They all agreed to eat healthier in the New Year after overindulging for Thanksgiving and Christmas, as well as overindulging in the last two family dinners.

Everyone wasn't due back to work until Tuesday. Trey's child care center was back open on Tuesday as well. Nonetheless, by 3:00

p.m., the family was ready to call it a day. Craig had fallen asleep on the couch. Chloe woke him up so they could go home. On Monday, the family rested in the comfort of their own homes. Monday turned out to be the quiet before the storm.

*****

Tuesday started as any normal workday. The family had no idea that Ms. Cooper had planned a visit to Trey's child care center with the police. Because the worker was from child protective service with court-ordered documents and was accompanied by the police, the childcare director was mandated to allow the worker to see James Jackson III without notifying his parents.

The director ushered everyone into a small conference room that was equipped to video record meetings. Once the teacher bought Trey into the conference room, the director pushed the record button. Ms. Cooper was allowed to question Trey in front of the childcare director and the police. She asked him if his parents touched him on the body parts she pointed to on a picture of a male child. She had pointed to the butt area on the picture. Trey said, "Yes. When my mommy and daddy take off or put on my clothes." She pointed to the penis on the picture. Trey said, "Yes. When my mommy and daddy give me a bath." She asked Trey if he was hungry at home sometimes. Trey said, "Yes. Before my mommy and daddy feed me, I am hungry." Due to past experiences, the director of the child care center did not let the worker know the meeting was video recorded. It was part of the child care center bylaws to video record all legal or government agency meetings with kids whose guardians were not present.

When JJ and Grace arrived home on Tuesday evening, they noticed another letter was taped to their door. They did not think much of the letter because of the previous ones they received. That evening, before going to bed, Grace felt an urgency to read the letter. She was stunned to see the letter was for a court hearing scheduled on Monday of the following week. The letter stated that in order to avoid kidnap charges, they were to bring James Jackson III to the hearing. JJ was coming out of the shower when Grace screamed for him to come. She was shaking so bad she could not talk. She handed the letter to JJ to read. JJ did not know what to say. He was just as stunned as Grace.

JJ decided to look at the security camera, which showed Ms. Cooper knocking on the door and ringing the doorbell around 9:15 a.m. with the police. The only words of comfort JJ could rationalize within his mind to say to Grace was, "It's going to be okay. The court will see that this is a big misunderstanding. How can we be given a court date when we haven't been charged with anything? This doesn't make sense. This has to be a mistake. Maybe it's a good thing we have a court date so we can put an end to this craziness."

"JJ, do you think we should inform the family so we can have support at the court hearing?"

"Grace, I think the judge will see there isn't any evidence against us and therefore end this craziness. I don't want the family to worry over something so foolish."

"JJ, I hope you are using wisdom."

JJ hunched his shoulders as he finished preparing for bed.

*****

JJ was concerned if they would make it to court on time. The Monday morning drive heading toward the downtown area was congested with stop and go traffic. They arrived thirty minutes prior to check-in. An hour after checking in with the bailiff, a tall slender lady called for the Jackson family waiting for courtroom 400. JJ raised his hand so the lady could see they were present. The lady approached the family, introducing herself as Mrs. Black, their court-appointed lawyer.

Grace shouted, "Lawyer! Why do we need a lawyer? What did we do?"

"According to the report from the child protective service, you are being charged with child neglect and child molestation."

"What the heck are you talking about!" shouted JJ. "We have never neglected or molested our child. Where is this coming from?"

"According to the report from child protective service, there were several complaints called into their hotline. A worker came to your home several times to follow up on the complaints. The worker was only allowed access on the initial visit. According to the worker, during the initial visit, your wife asked her where she lived and stated she has ways of finding out. Also, your wife instructed your son not to answer any questions. Because the worker was not allowed access in your home to follow up on the complaints, the worker had no other recourse than to visit with James Jackson III at his child care center on Tuesday, January 3. James Jackson III stated that he was touched by his mom and dad inappropriately in the butt area, as well as in his genital area. The child states he is not given enough food and is always hungry."

A court sheriff deputy called the Jackson family name as the lawyer was explaining the complaints against them. The lawyer waved the deputy in their direction. The deputy stated their hearing would be called next, and that he was there to take James Jackson III to childcare. JJ and Grace argued that Trey was to stay with them, and they did not give the deputy permission to take him to childcare. The deputy stated it was court-ordered. Mrs. Black assured JJ and Grace they would address this with the court when they were called into session.

The bailiff from room 400 called for the Jackson family. Mrs. Black escorted her clients into the courtroom. She asked them to have a seat as she spoke to the bailiff. The judge had his head down, reading through papers in a manila folder as the Jacksons entered the courtroom. The judge looked up and asked if the Jacksons were present. The bailiff stated, "Yes, Your Honor. The Jacksons are present." Mrs. Black asked JJ and Grace to stand.

"Are they represent with counsel?"

"Yes, Your Honor. The Jacksons' counsel is here as well."

"Is child protective service counsel present?"

"Yes, Your Honor. Child Protective counsel is present."

"Please have all parties approach the stand."

Mrs. Black instructed JJ and Grace where to go. JJ and Grace did not see Ms. Cooper in the courtroom and was confused since she was the one who wrote all the nasty allegations against them. The judge read out loud the complaints against the Jacksons and asked them how they would plead. JJ and Grace both stated that they were not guilty because the complaints were false. Mrs. Black informed JJ and Grace that this was not a trial, and they were to only answer the judge's questions without pleading their case.

The judge asked child protective service's counsel, "Has the child been seen by a medical professional for the molestation?" The child protective counsel stated that a report from the medical professional would be available in the next court hearing. The judge asked if the Jacksons' relative home had been approved for the care of the child. Child Protective counsel answered, "Yes, Your Honor." The judge asked the child protective service's lawyer why the files were missing documents showing the approval of John Jackson's home, as well as the professional reports confirming the evidence of molestation. The lawyer stated it was an oversight due to the time rush of the hearing date. JJ and Grace did not know what was going on. They both asked Mrs. Black. She instructed them to remain silent.

The judge turned to JJ and Grace. "Mr. and Mrs. Jackson, I hope you understand the seriousness of the charges against you. It is of your best interest to follow all the guidelines outlined by child protective service and this court in order to gain back the care of your child. The court is ordering you both to attend parenting classes, as well as no less than ten psychological sessions. The court is ordering psychological counseling for James Jacksons III. The court would like to see in the file by the next hearing the medical professional's report, the parenting class certificate of completion, and the psychological reports. The court is ordering James III to be placed in the care of his uncle John Jackson with monitor visitations from the parents. The next court hearing has been scheduled to take place in three months."

JJ yelled, "Your Honor, please! You have this all wrong. My wife and I have not done anything to our child. Please do not remove our child from our home and place him with a stranger. He doesn't know my uncle John. I just met him myself approximately three months ago. My uncle John was recently living in a sober living facility. How can you place my child in this stranger's home?"

Grace broke down and cried nonstop until she hyperventilated. The paramedic had to be called.

"Mr. Jackson, child services has approved the home of your uncle, as well as deemed him a fit person to care for your child. Please follow the court orders, and I will see you back here in three months."

JJ started screaming, "Where is my son!"

The sheriff deputy handcuffed JJ until he calmed down. Due to safety reasons, because of their hysterical outbursts, JJ and Grace were not allowed to see Trey. Mrs. Black gave them the name and phone number of the childcare worker assigned to their case. She instructed them to contact the worker to arrange monitor visits.

After taking the information from Mrs. Black, JJ told her, "I do not know who hired you, but I am firing you."

Grace did not want to leave the court without her son. The paramedic was able to stabilize her breathing but feared she would hyperventilate again if she did not calm down. JJ told Grace they needed to go to the car so they could call his mom. Grace did not want to leave the court without her son; however, JJ was able to convince her to go with him to the car so they could talk in private, free of the noise inside the building.

JJ put the phone on speaker as he dialed his mom. Rose became hysterical as well, when she suddenly realized it wasn't helping JJ or Grace.

"JJ, hold on and let me call Craig. He will know what to do. JJ, I need for you and Grace to stay calm. I know it's not an easy thing to do right now, but Trey needs us all to be strong for him. We need to think with a clear head and remain well so we can get him back home where he belongs."

Rose explained to Craig that JJ was on hold, and she wanted to connect him to their call. Craig agreed.

"JJ, please let Craig know what just happened."

JJ explained to Craig the best he could with the limited information and understanding he and Grace had about this whole ordeal.

"JJ, I know this is a very traumatic experience for you and Grace, but I promise you, we will get Trey back home. The only way to fight child protective service is with a good attorney, not the court-appointed lawyer, whose only purpose is to inform you on how to follow the guidelines of the court and child protective service. This will not be an overnight fight; therefore, you and Grace will have to find strength in God like never before. You will have to join together in your relationship with God and trust that he is with Trey, keeping him safe. As difficult as this is to do, I need you two to calmly go to the child service office within the court building to ask for a monitor visit with Trey before you leave the court. Explain to Trey the best you can that he will temporarily be staying with your uncle John. It's important to help Trey feel as comfortable about this horrific, scary moment as possible. I know an attorney who handles cases dealing with children who were wrongfully taken from their family by child protective service. I will give him a call now. I will call you this evening, JJ, to give you an update on the attorney and to hear how your visit went with Trey."

"Okay, Craig. Thank you."

Grace felt calmer after hearing what Craig said. Rose thanked Craig before hanging up. JJ and Grace were able to visit with Trey before they left the court. They both explained to Trey that his visit with John was temporarily until they both work through a misunderstanding with the court. They told Trey to let the school and social worker know if he felt sick or was hurt or hungry. They promised to visit him soon. Trey appeared to be in good spirit with the news, which helped them both to remain calm.

As promised, Craig called JJ around 7:00 p.m.

"JJ, how are you and Grace holding up?"

"We are doing better than earlier today. It's hard to think of our child in the care of that monster. Craig, can I put you on speaker so Grace can hear?"

"Yes, please do. I talked to Attorney Blair Norwood. He agreed to take your case. I took the liberty of giving him your phone number. I will text his phone number to you. I shared with him all that you had told me about the case. The attorney said based on what I told him, this is an open-and-shut case. He will have it back in court within a month and guarantees it will be thrown out of court. He needs you and Grace to call him tomorrow morning at 8:30 a.m. so he can start on the case."

"What would we do without you, Craig? I am so grateful to God for you. Thank you again. Good night, Craig."

"Good night, JJ and Grace."

*****

JJ and Grace had taken a couple of days off work to deal with the legal issues in bringing Trey back home. JJ called attorney Norwood exactly at 8:30 a.m. He informed the attorney that he was on speaker phone so that his wife could be a part of the conversation.

"Good morning, Mr. and Mrs. Jackson. I would like to record our conversation in order to represent you both with accuracy. Please share with me all your interactions with child protective service from the beginning to the date of your court hearing."

JJ and Grace provide the attorney with all the details leading up to the hearing, as well as what happened at the hearing. Grace suddenly remembered why Ms. Cooper looked familiar and shared the information with JJ and the attorney.

"Ms. Cooper was at the repast for Mother Baker. She was seated at the same table as Craig's cousin Ralph and his daughter, April."

"Mr. and Mrs. Jackson, I will have my staff do background checks on John, April, and Ms. Cooper. In the meantime, I need to have your son examined by his primary care doctor for sexual abuse, as well as by an urgent care doctor provided by CPS. My assistant will be present for the exams. I need to request a written affidavit from your son's child care center for their observation of child neglect or abuse, as well as for the minutes of the meeting child protective service had with your son at the center. Also, I will request a copy of the child protective service worker's affidavit on why they got involved with your family and why the child was removed. I will request a copy of the petition the child protective service's filed with the court. Immediately following this meeting, I will email to you, Mr. Jackson, a consent form authorizing me to represent you and Mrs. Jackson. You both will need to electronically sign the form so I can legally start the process. Once the consent form has been signed, I will request an urgent contest hearing with the court. Therefore, we all need to work in a timely matter with replying to each other. I will need the address of your child's care center, as well as the name and address of his primary doctor.

"Mr. and Mrs. Jackson, please be at peace in knowing my firm will do all that it can in reuniting you with your son as soon as possible. In the meantime, make sure you set up the monitor visits with your son so that he remains calm during this ordeal."

"Thank you, Attorney Norwood. My wife and I will make sure you receive all the information and signed documents per your request."

After electronically signing the consent form and emailing the attorney the information he requested, JJ did a group text to his family requesting a 7:00-p.m. virtual online meeting so he could bring everyone up-to-date on the case. Everyone immediately replied, accepting the time for the meeting. JJ set up the online virtual meeting using each of his family's email address so they would receive their online invite.

Grace called Ms. Green, the caseworker assigned to the case, to set up the monitor visits. She was able to schedule visits from 4:00 p.m. to 5:00 p.m. three times a week. The caseworker sent a request to John Jackson to bring Trey into the child protective service's office by 3:45 p.m. for his visits on Mondays, Wednesdays, and Fridays. John confirmed the worker's visit request for Trey.

After dinner, JJ and Grace logged into the online team meeting site. Within a five-minute time period, the family all joined the meeting. JJ shared with the family the status of the case and his meeting with Attorney Norwood. The family offered to assist in any way they could. Grace informed the family about why Ms. Cooper looked familiar to her. The family was curious as to the type of relationship Ms. Cooper had with Craig's cousin Ralph's family. Chloe offered to snoop around by asking other family members. Craig cautioned her to be careful and to not meet with anyone who closely associated with Ralph. The family ended their meeting with a prayer.

The next day, Attorney Norwood called JJ to schedule a face-to-face evening meeting with him and Grace. Because the law office was near the downtown area, Attorney Norwood suggested it would be easier for him to meet with the Jacksons at their home. The Jackson's home was in the direction of where the attorney lived. JJ was elated and asked the attorney if he would like to have dinner with him and Grace. The attorney accepted JJ's invite.

Upon his arrival at 6:00 p.m., JJ offered him a glass of wine or a nonalcoholic beverage. Attorney Norwood handed JJ and Grace one of his business cards before asking the kind of beverage he had available. The attorney settled for a fruit spritzer made with sparkling water, crust of fresh fruit, agave, and a mint leaf. Grace set the table as JJ prepared the spritzers. Grace had prepared a roasted chicken, butter mashed potatoes, fresh fried corn with green bell peppers, sautéed asparagus, and dinner rolls.

The attorney did not want his first in-person meeting with the Jacksons to be at the court hearing. He expressed his gratitude for them inviting him to dinner. His gratitude was further expressed with compliments to Grace on her cooking skills. He informed the Jacksons that the court had accepted his appeal for an urgent contest hearing, and that the hearing was set for three weeks from the date. Grace began to cry with joy.

After dinner, the attorney requested thirty more minutes of their time to go over the case. He wanted them to enjoy their meal without all the legal talk. He assured them that everything was going as planned with the case. After dinner, they all sat in the family room.

"Well, Mr. and Mrs. Jackson, a lot has transpired in the last couple of days. My firm has been busy on your behalf. I understand you have a monitored visit with James III tomorrow at 4:00 p.m.?"

"Yes," stated JJ. Grace nodded her head in agreement with JJ.

"Your son has a busy schedule tomorrow. He has a 10:00-a.m. doctor's appointment with his primary doctor and a 1:30 p.m. appointment with a doctor chosen by child protective service. The caseworker Ms. Green will be the person taking James III to his appointments. As promised, my assistant will be present during the medical appointments. Each doctor's report will be made available forty-eight hours after each appointment. My assistant will pick up copies of the reports. The director at your son's child care center will provide us with a signed affidavit of the meeting child protective service had with James III at the school, as well as an observation on your son's wellness. The director will also provide us with a video recording of the meeting. A background check has been ordered for John Jackson and April Jackson. However, we are not sure of April's current last name. She and John are listed as married in the foster care system; yet we cannot find a marriage certificate on file. Child protective service has John and April listed in their report as James III's only living relatives. They do not state the source of this information in their report.

"Do you have any questions for me?"

"Yes. The court ordered Grace and me to complete parenting classes, as well as attend no less than ten psychological sessions. Is it mandatory for us to do these sessions and class?"

"No. What the judge ordered is routine in every child protective care case. The judge is under the assumption that the protective service protocol has been followed and there is now a reason to fix the risk of maltreatment. I will show the court that the proper protocol was not followed and your son was removed based on falsified documents completed by Ms. Cooper, who is married to April's brother, Ralph Cooper Jr. Because no marriage certificate was found on John and April, it is believed April's last name is Cooper as well. Which means the foster care license attained by John and April Jackson was approved based on fraudulent information."

"This is good news!" shouted JJ.

"It's important to keep this information confidential from the caseworkers as you are visiting with your son. We don't want them to cover up the errors they made in this case. We need the judge to see it as is. This is how we win our case."

"Understood. Thank you."

"Well, tomorrow is another busy day. Thank you for dinner. I will keep in touch. Have a good evening."

"You as well."

JJ and Grace escorted Attorney Norwood to the door. Grace and JJ were so happy about the news they received that they embraced each other as they whispered in unison, "Thank you, Jesus" over and over again.

*****

JJ and Grace arrived at 3:50 p.m. for their monitor visit with Trey. They were taken to a small room that contained a rectangle table with four chairs. As they approached the room, they noticed a long window to see inside the room. Once they entered the room, they noticed a mirror on the opposite side of the outside window. It made them feel like criminals who were about to be interrogated as the police looked through the window from outside the room.

Trey was bought in the room at exactly 4:00 p.m. A large male person grabbed one of the chairs from the table and sat inside the room near the door. JJ and Grace had to make sure their feeling of being uncomfortable with the setup was not felt by Trey.

Trey ran to them, shouting mommy and daddy. JJ picked up his son and hugged and kissed him over and over again. Grace told JJ she wanted to give Trey some sugary kisses too. Grace asked Trey, "Are you having fun at Uncle John's house?"

"I don't have any toys to play with. I like watching the cartoons on TV."

"Are you going to school yet?"

"Uncle John says I can go to school next week."

"Do you like the food you eat?"

"I eat hotdogs with barbecue beans every day. Sometimes I have peanut butter and jelly sandwich."

"What do you drink?"

"I drink water."

"You don't have any milk?"

"No."

"Are there other kids for you to play with?"

"No. I stand in my room by myself."

"When do you come out your room?"

"When I go to the bathroom next to my room."

"Do you come out your room to eat?"

"No. I eat in my room."

"What furniture do you have in your room?"

"I have a little bed and a little table and a little chair and a little TV."

"Is there a window in your room?"

"Yes. It's at the top of the wall. I cannot see out of it. I can hear the kids playing outside."

JJ and Grace took turns hugging their son. The man sitting at the door took notes as he sat in silence, monitoring their visit. JJ and Grace wondered what he was recording on the notepad. They weren't doing anything other than talking to their son.

The time went fast. At exactly 5:00 p.m., Trey was removed from the room as JJ and Grace were asked to exit. The Jacksons asked if they could bring their son a toy and restaurant fast food to their next visit. Per the receptionist, two small toys and food were allowed.

On the ride home, JJ and Grace discussed their visit with Trey. Although, they weren't happy with Trey being with John, they were both happy he was not exposed to anything other than a lot of cartoons.

JJ and Grace texted an updated to the family about their visit with Trey. In JJ's group text, he let everyone know that Trey looked well. That he was in good spirit and was basically kept in a room all day to watch TV. This would change when he was allowed to go to school next week. The worker would transport him to and from school because John didn't have a reliable car, and they were not allowed to remove him from his current school before the next hearing. The family texted their feedback and support.

The day of court had arrived. JJ and Grace were up early with little sleep the night before. Rose offered to pick up JJ and Grace for court. She knew they both would be too nervous to focus on the road. She and Janice arrived at JJ's house at 5:00 a.m. for the two-hour drive. She wanted to allow extra time in case of traffic. Chloe, her husband, Robert, and Craig drove together to court. After checking in with the bailiff, Attorney Norwood greeted the family at court and provided a briefing of the case. The family asked the attorney if Trey was at court.

"Yes. He is in childcare behind the judge's chambers."

At 10:00 a.m., the court bailiff called for the Jackson family to come to courtroom 400. Five minutes after entering the courtroom, the judge asked if all parties were present. All parties acknowledged their presence.

"Attorney Norwood, you have the burden of proof, so present your case."

"Thank you, Your Honor. I would like to start with the investigating worker's, Ms. Cooper, affidavit. In the affidavit, Ms. Cooper states she asked for hotline complaint number 853 to be assigned to her. She further states that because of the severity of the case, she asked that the local police accompany her on the wellness check. According to Ms. Cooper, the child had severe visual bruises on his back, legs, and arm. Because the police were detaining the father due to his violent outburst, they were not able to see the bruises. Ms. Cooper states her busy scheduled is the reason she did not submit a petition to the court to have the child remove for two months. Your Honor, I would like to submit a copy of child protective service's complaint number 853, which states a caller identifying themselves as a close friend of the Jacksons who is concerned about the Jacksons' son, Trey, because his parents only feed him once a day. Also, I would like to submit a copy of a second affidavit file on complaint number 853 by Ms. Cooper's supervisor, Mr. Brown, who accompanied Ms. Cooper on the wellness check.

"Mr. Brown was not aware that Ms. Cooper had submitted a petition to the court on a case that was closed. According to Mr. Brown's affidavit, Ms. Cooper was a trainee of six weeks at the time of complaint number 853. For this reason, he accompanied Ms. Cooper on all her complaint investigations. Mr. Brown states Ms. Cooper went upstairs with Mrs. Jackson to bring her son downstairs for the wellness check. Mr. Jackson remained downstairs with him and the police. Mr. Brown wrote that he asked Mr. Jackson a few questions about his son's eating habits. According to Mr. Brown, Mr. Jackson states his son eats breakfast, lunch, and two snacks at his child's care center Monday through Friday. On these days, he only eats dinner at home. As Mr. Brown was going to ask Mr. Jackson about his son's eating habit on the weekend, Ms. Cooper came back down the stairs in a hurry to leave. According to Mr. Brown, his attention went immediately to Ms. Cooper and asked her where the child was. Ms. Cooper stated she did the wellness check, and they could leave. On the ride back to the office, Mr. Brown asked Ms. Cooper if she followed protocol for the wellness check and if the outcome was well. Ms. Cooper stated the wellness check went well. Therefore, Mr. Brown closed out complaint number 853.

"Six weeks after complaint number 853, Ms. Cooper became a permanent employee and no longer needed her supervisor to oversee her work. Two weeks after becoming a permanent employee, Ms. Cooper files a petition with the courts to have the Jacksons' son, Trey, removed from their home due to sexual and physical abuse. Ms. Cooper, lacking in experience, did not know the court would question the missing supporting documents, such as the medical report, as well as pictures supporting visual bruises on the child's body.

"Your Honor, based on this evidence alone, the court could clearly see that imminent danger was not presented or validated by child protective service toward complaint number 853. All investigating reports attained after the child was removed from the family home shows no evidence of physical or sexual abuse. The child James Jackson III should have never been removed from his home and given to stranger whom he had just met when he has a family who is here today in this court, who also would have been available to care for the child should this had been a case of imminent danger."

The judge asked attorney Norwood, "Does Ms. Cooper personally know this family?"

"Your Honor, Ms. Cooper know of this family, but she doesn't personally know them. She is the daughter-in-law of Mr. Jackson's stepfather's cousin."

"I see."

The judge asked the child protective service's lawyer if she would like to contest the evidence presented by attorney Norwood.

"No, Your Honor. I concur. There is no imminent danger."

"Okay. Based on these findings, I rule that James Jackson III be returned to the care of his parents immediately."

Shouts of joy rang out in the courtroom from the family. Attorney Norwood escorted the family to the court's child care department to pick up Trey. JJ picked his son up into his arms and sobbed as he held him close.

"Daddy, are you okay? Why are you crying?"

"I am happy to see you and happy you are coming home with us today."

"Daddy, I don't have to stay with Uncle John anymore?"

"No, son, you don't."

Trey hugged his daddy tight before turning to his mom to hug her tight as well. The family took turns hugging and kissing Trey. Before exiting the court building, the family thanked Attorney Norwood for a job well done.

The family went to JJ's home to celebrate. Craig ordered pizza from Trey's favorite pizza parlor. Grace made a salad. Robert and Chloe picked up items from the local market to make ice cream sundaes. The family enjoyed Trey's return home together.

"To God be the glory, for the works of God have been manifested!" shouted Craig.

"Amen!" shouted the family.

As the family continued to enjoy one another, everyone noticed how close Craig and Rose were sitting and how they would touch each other as they talked.

*****

As the first quarter of the New Year came to a close, Janice reflected back on all that had happened since her first session with Dr. Ruth one year ago. She was ready to share with the family and Dr. Ruth about the new love interest in her life.

Janice met Glen at the clinic where she worked. He was the client of another physical therapist. Glen was a coach at the university near Janice's home. He injured his ankle while jogging one morning in the park during winter break from school. Glen's left foot went into a pot hole as he was distracted by a barking dog. Glen's twisted ankle immediately swelled to the size of a grapefruit. Although he did not break a bone, his ankle hurt every time he stood for a long period of time.

Glen was five years Janice's senior. He and Janice were kindred spirits. He was engaged once but never married. His fiancée cheated on him with his best friend. The hurt from this experience caused Glen to not easily trust another female.

Like Janice, Glen talked to a psychologist weekly to help him deal with the hurt and betrayal he received from someone he loved. Although Glen's counseling ended nearly six months ago, he was not in a hurry to find love again. Glen would occasionally date women who were not looking for a serious relationship because he was not looking for a serious relationship. His feelings changed when he met Janice. Glen suddenly realized he could feel again after being numb for years.

Janice also realized the hurt that blocked her from feeling joy was gone. Janice felt like a young giddy school girl when she was around Glen. Her stomach was bubbly, and she couldn't stop smiling. Although Glen had only been exclusively dating Janice for three months, he was asking to meet her family. Glen introduced Janice to his family after one month of dating her. Janice promised Glen that she would introduce him to her family at their next family dinner in two weeks.

Janice decided it was time to tell Rose about Glen. She called her mom on her lunch break, asking if she could treat her to dinner.

"Sure, Janice. I would love to have dinner with you. We haven't seen each other much after you moved out the house seven weeks ago. What is the occasion?"

"It's nothing to be alarmed about. I want to talk with you about someone I met and have been dating for three months."

Rose was happy Janice could not see the huge smile she had on her face.

"How about we order food and have dinner at my house so we can talk in private?"

"That sounds good, Mom. I will be at your house at 5:30 p.m."

"Okay, Janice. Sounds good."

Janice texted her mom at 5:00 p.m. to say she would be fifteen minutes late because she ordered food for pickup rather than delivery. Janice ordered grilled salmon, baby red potatoes, steamed broccoli, and Italian salad with dinner rolls from her mom's favorite restaurant.

The food was steaming hot when Janice arrived at her mom's house. The restaurant had packaged the food containers in a throwaway thermal bag. As they ate, Janice talked about Glen and his family. Rose was surprised to hear how fast the relationship between Glen and Janice developed to the exclusive status. She knew counseling had helped Janice with the family, but she did not know the magnitude of the change. This explained Janice's sudden desire to have her own place.

Rose was very happy with the new Janice. Rose felt Janice was strong enough to handle the change that had taken place in her life as well. She informed Janice that she and Craig had been secretly seeing each other.

"Mom, you and Craig dating are no secret. The family saw the sparks between you two the day we celebrated Trey's return home. But I am personally happy you two are back together."

They both laughed out loud.

"Well, Mom, it's getting late."

Rose looked at the clock; it was 8:00 p.m.

"Let me walk you to the door."

Janice hugged her mom before leaving. Rose shouted, "I will see you tomorrow in passing Dr. Ruth's office!"

Janice shouted back to her mom before getting in her car, "Yes! This is our last session."

*****

Dr. Ruth called Janice into her office.

"Hello, Janice. It is good to see you again. You are still glowing. A lot has transpired in this past year of conversing with you. It is always good to see my clients blossom."

"Thank you, Dr. Ruth. It feels good to blossom with a glow."

"With you and your mom's permission, I video recorded the first family group session you had with your mom and the last family session. As promised, here is a copy of the two sessions. It shows the growth between you and your mom as a family, as well as an individual. For this reason, I label this video 'With God, All Things Are Possible.' Let's use this last session for you to share the glow. How do you define your glow?"

"Dr. Ruth, I define my glow as spiritual fruit. The Bible tells us in Galatians 5:22–23, 'The fruit of the Spirit is love, joy, peace, long-suffering, gentleness, goodness, faith, meekness, temperance: against such there is no law.' As you know, Dr. Ruth, I was lost, broken, and filled with despair when I came to you. In my mind, because of the magnitude of despair, I did not see my life without it. It became my friend and grew to become my husband. We were intimate partners. The beautiful thing about God's love is that it's working on the inside of me. It was silent and gentle. With God's love, I did not feel the instant sharpness as I felt with hurt and pain. I did not know how to recognize his love because it did not pierce my spirit in the same manner as pain. As I spent time with God through meditation, in prayer, reading his Word, and listening to sermons, I began to notice that the pain and hurt was losing its hold on me. I woke up one morning and realized that piercing feeling of pain was gone. My heart was open to love. I know it did not happen overnight; yet I do not know in what interval it did happen.

"I discussed with you in our last session my relationship with Glen. I do not believe Glen would be in my life now had I not been open to giving counseling a chance. Counseling helped in ushering me back into the presence of God. For these reasons, I am truly grateful to you, Dr. Ruth, and to God for his unconditionally love. I now understand his love was always with me because in my darkness, I could still see and talk about his goodness even though I felt his goodness was detached from me. Last week, I was reading the prophetic word written by Paul in first Corinthians 13:4–8: 'Love is patient, love is kind, and love is not jealous. Love does not brag and is not arrogant. Love does not act unbecomingly; it does not seek its own. Love is not provoked and does not take into account a wrong suffered. Love does not rejoice in unrighteousness; it rejoices with the truth. Love bears all things; believe all things and hopes all things. Love endures all things. Love never fails.'"

"Janice, thank you, and God bless you. I would like to end our session with Psalms 23: 'The Lord is my shepherd; I shall not want. He maketh me to lie down in green pastures: he leadeth me beside the still waters. He restoreth my soul: he leadeth me in the paths of righteousness for his name's sake, Yea, though I walk through the valley of the shadow of death, I will fear no evil: for thou art with me; thy rod and thy staff they comfort me. Thou preparest a table before me in the presence of mine enemies: thou anointest my head with oil; my cup runneth over. Surely goodness and mercy shall follow me all the days of my life: and I will dwell in the house of the Lord forever.'"

"Amen," declared Janice. "Bye, Dr. Ruth."

Janice passed her mom in the waiting room as she was exiting. Janice hugged and kissed her mom as she exited. Dr. Ruth came out to call Rose into her office.

"Hello, Rose. Have a seat."

"Hello, Dr. Ruth."

"Let's use this last session to talk about your relationship with Craig. Last week, you ended your session stating that you were developing feelings for Craig."

"Yes, Dr. Ruth, this is true. I would like to correct the statement I made last week. I am not developing feelings for Craig. I have developed feelings for Craig."

"Okay, past tense. Let's talk about your feelings for Craig. What has transpired that allowed you to know you have feelings for him?"

"Well, Dr. Ruth, it was a series of events that happened. These events allowed me to feel the love within I have for Craig. The first event happened at the hospital during Craig's mother's surgery. One of Craig's cousin verbally attacked me for coming to the hospital to support Craig and Chloe. The cousin told me that I was no longer a family member and should leave. Craig defended me by telling his cousin he was not allowed to attack his ex-wife of twenty years and the mother of his only child. Craig told his cousin to leave if he had a problem with me being there. It meant something special to see Craig momentarily put aside his own grief to come to my aid. Suddenly, I realized this is who Craig is and always has been. For some reason, I appreciated it more at that moment then I have throughout our marriage.

"Another event happened when Craig was in great emotional pain after his mother died; yet he found the strength to plan her homegoing service and her repast. He did a wonderful job making sure her homegoing was a celebration in memory of her love and spirit. Thirdly, when my ex-husband, James Sr.'s, younger brother, John, found a way to get in touch with my son, JJ, and requested to build a relationship him, Craig gave JJ some wonderful words of wisdom. And although JJ did not follow the words of wisdom, which ended up with his uncle John using child protective service to remove JJ's son, Trey, from his home and temporarily place him in John's home, Craig found JJ a good attorney.

"Craig has prayed with the family and for the family. Since Craig moved back in town with our daughter Chloe and her husband, he has reclaimed his place as head of this family by stepping up and taking the lead. Watching Craig in operation over the last few months brought back memories as to why I married him. The difference between now from when I first married Craig is that now, my heart is open to love. I am no longer carrying the hurt and pain I had endured from my first love, James Sr. For twenty years, I was an empty shell married to this wonderful man that I could not celebrate or appreciate in the way he desires. Yet he loved me in spite of my lack thereof with an unconditional love. Recently, because I was feeling so bad and guilty about not reciprocating the love I received from Craig, I asked him to forgive me so I can now freely love him without guilt. Craig and I are engaged and plan on remarrying in three months. I can honestly say that I am in love with Craig. Dr. Ruth, it feels good."

"Rose, I am so elated to see your heart is no longer suffocating from the emotional blockage caused by pain and hurt. I don't think it was by accident that Craig found his way back into your life. The Bible declares in Romans 8:28 that all things worked together for good to them that love God. In all the pain you carried for years, your love for God was steadfast. You raised your kids on godly principles. There is no fear in love, for perfect love cast out fear. I believe you and Craig's love have been made perfect through Christ, who strengthens you. Be blessed in love, Rose."

"Thank you, Dr. Ruth. I will send you an invite to the wedding. Have a good day. Bye."

"Bye, Rose. You as well."

Rose left her last session with Dr. Ruth feeling rejuvenated and happy.

*****

Rose woke up early on Saturday to go for her morning jog before planning Sunday dinner with the family. Rose would host the dinner at her place, as well as cater the food. She called for Josey as she gathered Josey's dog collar and leash. Josey ran to the door waging her tail with excitement.

As Rose was jogging, her thoughts reflected on her best friend, Barbara. She thought it would be good to invite Barbara to the family dinner. Barbara was the reason she met Craig and was the person who suggested Dr. Ruth. Besides, Rose felt it was time for Craig and his cousin Barbara to mend their relationship. Craig could not continue to hold his cousin Barbara accountable for not becoming a mediator in their marriage after she asked for a divorce.

Because Rose was so deep in thought, she jogged a little longer than normal. Josey was panting for water when they arrived home. Rose called Barbara before heading upstairs to shower.

"Good morning, Rose."

"Good morning, Barbara. I hope you do not mind me calling you so early in the morning on a Saturday. I know you are an early riser and would be up."

"It's okay, Rose. I'm sitting on my deck, having a cup of coffee."

"I called to invite you to the family Sunday dinner tomorrow. As you know, Craig is living with Chloe and her husband, and I have invited him as well. It would mean the world to me if you both were here."

"Rose, I would love to come. Besides, I'm not the one angry with him. He stopped speaking to me. What time should I be there, and do you need me to bring a dish?"

"Everyone will arrive around 2:00 p.m., and there is no need for you to bring a dish. There will be plenty of food. Thank you for asking."

"Okay, Rose. I will see you tomorrow at 2:00 p.m."

Rose told Barbara to enjoy her cup of coffee before hanging up the phone. Rose decided to go back to the original family dinner theme: A Soul Food Gathering.

After showering, Rose made a list of items to purchase on her cell phone's quick memo app. With her phone in hand, Rose headed out the door to the farmer's market. Two hours later, she returned back home with an assortment of baked items from the farmer's market bakery and bags of fresh food to-go with items she already had in her cabinet.

Rose began to prepare the food items that took the longest to prepare. She would store the cooked items in serving dishes that could be heated in the oven or in the microwave. By five o'clock, Rose was tired from cooking and setting the serving table with tableware. She spent the rest of her evening reading and giving God thanks.

Sunday afternoon, Rose was finishing up transferring the cooked food from pots into serving dishes when the doorbell rang at 1:30 p.m. *Someone is early*, Rose thought as she went to the door. It was Craig, Chloe, and Robert at the door.

"Sorry, Mom. Dad couldn't wait at home any longer."

"It's okay, Chloe. I am glad you all are here. Come in."

Craig and Rose looked at each other and almost greeted with a kiss when they realized the kids were there, and they hadn't told them yet that they were dating again. Rose asked Chloe to help her get beverages for everyone. The rest of the family arrived on time at 2:00 p.m.

Everyone was frozen in thought as Janice arrived with a male companion. She looked at her family and giggled.

"Everyone, this is Glen. Glen and I are dating."

Everyone took turns greeting Glen and welcoming him to the family dinner.

Barbara was the last to arrive at 2:20 p.m. Craig was surprised and elated to see his cousin was invited. He took her by the hand and pulled her toward him as he wrapped his arms around her. He whispered, "Please accept my apology" as they embraced in a hug.

Barbara whispered back in Craig's ear, "There is nothing to apologize about. All is forgiven. You are still my favorite cousin."

Rose was eager to get dinner started. She asked Chloe and Janice to help her as she set the dining table and placed the food on the serving table. Rose called for everyone to come into the dining room. She asked Craig if he would bless the food before they sit. Something quickened in Barbara's spirit as she watched Craig and Rose's interaction with each other. She began to smile. Rose looked at Barbara and knew her secret was no longer a secret.

Craig prayed for the blessing of the food, as well as for each person present. Everyone looked up at him as he kept thanking God for Rose. Once they all were settled with their plate of food, Rose invited everyone to use this time, as they ate, to share whatever was on their mind. Janice spoke first.

"I would like to share with everyone that Glen and I have been exclusively dating for over three months. You all will be seeing more of him at our family gatherings."

Everyone shouted welcome to Glen. Glen thanked everyone for the warm welcome and expressed how he was looking forward to getting to know everyone. Chloe spoke next.

"Robert and I would like everyone to know we are expecting our first child in six months. We are pregnant."

Everyone laughed out loud when Craig shouted, "How did that happen!"

"What I mean is, I have been living with them since the passing of Mother Baker, and I did not suspect a thing."

"Dad, that's because you have been so busy drooling over Mom that you haven't noticed much of anything else."

The laughter started again.

"Okay," Barbara declared, "spill the beans, you two. It was obvious to me. The manner in which Rose asked Craig to bless the food, something is going on."

"You all are correct in your observation. Rose and I are engaged. The wedding is taking place in three months. It will be a small inti- mate wedding here at the house in the backyard. We will have fancy tables and chairs under a huge tent for the reception. A portable dance floor large enough to hold fifty people and a separate decorate area for the actual wedding."

JJ stood up to speak. "I would like to give honor to God for his love, his mercy, and his grace. As a family of believers who love God and try to follow his principles outlined for us in the instruc- tion Book of Life called the Holy Bible, we don't always get it right. Sometimes we go left when we clearly hear him tell us to go right. Sometimes we are met with calamity when we have not wronged anyone. Sometimes we still have to feel the pain of life when we pray for betterment. Sometimes we have to endure hatred and jealously from people who we are showing love. Nevertheless, in spite of all we go through, God is still God. The Lord is our Shepherd. Yeah, though we walk through the valley of the shadow of death, God is with us. His mercy shall follow us all the days of our life. We will rejoice in the good and bad times. We will praise him in the good and bad times.

"Craig, I am so happy you are back home where you belong. You have been a wonderful father to me and Janice. Chloe, I am so happy you and Robert are expecting your first child. Janice, my heart is so full when I look at you. Your life is a story of hope that needs to be told. Your story is what helped me get through my dark- est hours when Trey was removed from our home. I questioned my relationship with God. I questioned God's love for me. My heart ached like never before, and I did not know how I was going to get through it. I wanted to physically hurt the people who was hurting me. As I reflected on the manifestable love of God in your life, it kept my head above water and in sound and sane mind. Because of our tribulations, my wife and I are stronger in our faith and are happy to announce we are also pregnant and are expecting our second child in seven months. To God be the glory."

ABOUT THE AUTHOR

Judy Owens is a mother, a grandmother, and a wife, who is currently living in California. She is an avid reader who has always desired to share her wisdom in print. Judy's love for reading began at the age of fifteen after reading her first book, *The Diary of Anne Frank*. Throughout the years, reading has taken Judy into a place of serenity, where she visions the world through someone's creative thoughts on print. Judy's hope is to enrich the life of the reader.

9 781638 852100